The Latter Rain:
Unleashing the Gifts for the End Time

Mariangeli Morauske

COPYRIGHT © 2025 by Mariángeli Morauske.

Mariángeli Morauske, MD, MACP., MAPM., Ch., affirms the moral right to be identified as the author of this work.
Edited by Mariangeli Morauske

Graphic design and composition: Mariangeli Morauske
Cover Design: Mariangeli Morauske
Top image: A.I., Not real people

Printed in the United States of America. All rights reserved.
Imprint: Published independently.

No part of this book may be reproduced, stored in a retrieval system, or transmitted in any form or by any means, electronic, mechanical, photocopying, recording, scanning, or otherwise, without the prior written permission of the author, except for short quotations used in critical reviews or articles. Permission can be requested by contacting the author by email at endtimessequence@aol.com.

Unless otherwise indicated, all quotations from Sacred Scripture are taken from the The King James Version present on the Bible Gateway matches the 1987 printing. Used by permission. All rights reserved.

Quotations from Ellen G. White are from the online collection of her writings available at www.egwwritings.org. Copyright © 2025 by the Ellen G. White Estate, Inc. Used by permission. All rights reserved.

English: Updated Edition
ISBN: 979-8-89965-954-6 Paperback

English: Updated Edition
ISBN: 979-8-89965-959-1 Paperback

Table of Contents

Dedication 7

A Word of Grace to the Reader 9

Preface 11

Prologue 1

Chapter 1 – The Gifts and the Church: The Body of Christ in Motion 3

Chapter 2: About Spiritual Gifts 19

Chapter 3: The Distribution of the Gifts 39

Chapter 4: Understanding Spiritual Gifts 71

Chapter 5: The Dynamics of Spiritual Gifts 85

Chapter 6: The Discovery of Spiritual Gifts 111

Chapter 7: Developing Spiritual Gifts 127

Chapter 8: The Discovery of Spiritual Gifts 141

   Questionnaire I 145

      Table I 147

   Questionnaire II 156

      Table II 170

Epilogue: Prepared for the Latter Rain 175

Meet The Author 179

Bibliography 182

Dedication

To my dear sister, **Jeanine Valenzuela,**

Your life is a living testimony of the grace and power of the Holy Ghost. I have always seen in you a genuine surrender, an unwavering faith, and a humble willingness to allow God to mold and develop the gifts He has placed in you.

Every word you speak, every act of love you perform, every moment you serve with passion and dedication, reflects the work of the Spirit in you. **Your gifts have not been kept, but multiplied for the glory of God and the building up of His Church.**

You have been a light, a voice of wisdom, and an instrument of blessing to those who have the privilege of knowing you. **Your spiritual sensitivity, discernment, and love for the Lord's work have impacted lives in ways that only heaven can measure.**

Today, with gratitude and admiration, I dedicate these words to you, **as a recognition of the faithfulness with which you have allowed the Holy Spirit to work out His purpose in you.** May God continue to guide you, strengthen your calling, and use your life as a channel of His glory.

A Word of Grace to the Reader

Dear Reader,

Though this work has been written with deep prayer, biblical conviction, and careful review, I recognize that it may still contain errors—whether grammatical, typographical, or interpretive. This book, like each of us, is a work in progress, refined over time and by the grace of God.

If you come across something that needs correction, I invite you to extend grace and to become a co-laborer in this mission. Please feel free to contact me at endtimessequence@aol.com. With humility and gratitude, I will review your insight, and—with your permission—honor your contribution in future editions.

Your participation enriches not only this book but also the shared mission of building up the Body of Christ. Together, in truth and love, we prepare for the outpouring of the Latter Rain.

With gratitude and expectancy,
Dr. Mariangeli Morauske

Preface

"Now concerning spiritual gifts, brethren, I would not have you ignorant" (1 Corinthians 12:1). With these forceful words, the Apostle Paul opens a door to one of the most powerful truths of the New Testament: the gifts of the Spirit are not an optional luxury, but an essential element in the Christian life and in the ultimate mission of the Church. At a time when materialism has stifled missionary urgency, and when the church struggles to stay on fire, the issue of spiritual gifts rises with renewed importance.

This book is not simply a doctrinal exposition. It is a calling, a preparation for the great outpouring of the Holy Spirit promised for the time of the end: the latter rain. In its pages you will not only find a clear definition of what spiritual gifts are, but you will also discover how to identify, develop and put them at the service of the body of Christ.

Here we retrace, in the light of the Bible and the inspired writings of Ellen G. White, the different charisms of the Holy Spirit, their relationship to the fruit of the Spirit, to natural talents, to ecclesiastical offices and to the common responsibilities of Christian life. We also warn of the dangerous proliferation of pseudo-gifts in the age of spiritual confusion, and we present biblical criteria for discerning the authenticity of a spiritual manifestation.

Each chapter has been written with a yearning to activate, strengthen, and align God's people with their ultimate mission: to preach the everlasting gospel to every nation, tribe, tongue, and people. This mission will not be completed with human strategies, but with the supernatural power of the Spirit acting through his gifts. When the Church awakens to this reality, the world will know the glory of God. The latter rain is not a distant future event: it is a pending experience, ready to fall on hearts empty of themselves and full of God.

May this book be for you an activation tool, a guide to discernment, and a fire that burns within you. Because the same Spirit who poured out power at Pentecost is ready to fill His people again. And you, are you ready to receive it?

Prologue

The heavens are about to open. In the latter-day scenario, the history of the world is hurtling toward its prophetic denouement, and in the midst of that final scenario, a lingering promise is heard: God will pour out his Holy Spirit as a latter rain on his faithful people. This is not just any rain. It is a glorious manifestation of divine power, which will come to empower, awaken, and activate the spiritual gifts that lie dormant in many hearts.

We live in a prophetic time. The shadows of relativism, spiritual drought and ecclesiastical apathy have obscured the passion for mission. And yet, God has not left his Church without resources. On the contrary, He has provided a spiritual arsenal, and the gifts of the Holy Ghost are an essential part of that heavenly provision. This work has been written to rescue that message, to rediscover the wonder of divine charisms and to equip each reader with the light and tools necessary to recognize, activate and multiply the gifts that God has entrusted to his children.

This book is not just another theory or a cold exposition of doctrinal concepts. It is an ardent, living, and urgent invitation to participate in the most powerful end-time experience: to be filled with the Spirit and to be used by Him. In these pages you will find a clear exposition of what spiritual gifts really are, how they are distinguished from talents,

The Latter Rain: Unleashing the Gifts for the End Time!

fruits, and responsibilities; how many there are, how they operate, and why they are critical to the unity, growth, and effectiveness of Christ's Church.

In addition, we will delve into the most glorious promises of Scripture, and explore the powerful connection between gifts and the latter rain. We will see that the final outpouring of the Spirit will not be a spontaneous miracle without preparation, but God's response to a Church that has awakened, that has discovered its gifts and has put them at the service of the Kingdom.

The Latter Rain is not an event of the future, it is a reality that begins today, in your life, in your willing heart, in your sincere desire to be part of the last great revival. It is time to prepare, to consecrate ourselves, and to let the Fire of heaven mold us for its work.

As you read, pray. As you discover, commit. And as you understand, allow the Holy Spirit to transform your life.

The sky is about to rain! And God wants to use you.

Chapter 1 – The Gifts and the Church: The Body of Christ in Motion

Imagine for a moment that Christ's Church is not simply a cold building or institution, but a living, vibrant body in which each person has a unique and vital function. Just as our human body needs all of its organs to work in harmony—for blood to flow from the heart in perfect coordination—so too does the Church depend on each of us to fulfill the mission to which we have been called. God's Word explains it clearly:

"For as the body is one, and hath many members, and all the members of that one body, being many, are one body: so also is Christ." (1 Corinthians 12:12).

This image of unity touches me deeply, because it reminds me that each of us has been equipped by the Holy Spirit with gifts that are not born of our natural talent or the result of human effort. They are divine gifts, manifestations of God's grace, given precisely to build up His people and accomplish His work on earth.

Since ancient times, the Bible has taught us about the nature of these spiritual gifts. They are not simply inherited skills or acquired skills, but supernatural abilities that God pours out on us for service within His Church.

Think of Moses, called by God to lead Israel out of Egypt, of Bezalel and Oholiab, gifted for the magnificent task of building the tabernacle, of Peter who, on the day of Pentecost, preached with transforming power, or of Paul, whose ministry of teaching and doctrinal formation profoundly marked the life of the Church. Each received not just a task, but a manifestation of the Spirit that enabled them to serve uniquely.

Paul offers us an orderly view of gifts, distinguishing between those of service (such as prophecy, teaching, exhortation, generosity, leadership, and mercy), supernatural (such as wisdom, knowledge, faith, healing, miracles, discernment, tongues, and interpretation of tongues), and ministerial (apostles, prophets, evangelists, pastors, and teachers). These gifts, far from being a closed list, are a testimony of God's infinite creativity to operate in the midst of His family.

As we reflect on the metaphor of the body, we remember that each member has an essential role:

"But now hath God set the members every one of them in the body, as it hath pleased him" (1 Corinthians 12:18).

The Latter Rain: Unleashing the Gifts for the End Time!

In the society of the ancient world, especially in the Greco-Roman context, life was hierarchical and each person occupied a fixed place. The early Church broke with this structure by proposing a community where the identity and value of each individual came from his or her belonging to Christ, all being equal and necessary. Today, however, we face challenges such as individualism, religious consumerism, and denominational fragmentation, which threaten to weaken that powerful image of unity.

Ellen G. White, in her book The Great Controversy, reminds us that God has endowed His Church with diverse talents, and each one is to be employed for His glory. God's work does not advance by the efforts of a few, but by the cooperation of all.

She further stresses the importance of using these gifts with humility and in absolute dependence on the Holy Spirit:

Also, in her book Steps to Christ, she said that the true success in God's work does not depend on human eloquence, but on the presence of the Holy Spirit in every effort.

These words encourage me to explore, with sincerity and openness, what is the gift God has entrusted to me and how I can put it to work to bless others. For when each member commits himself to act according to the grace received, the Church becomes a united and vigorous organism, in which interdependence becomes the most powerful manifestation of Christ's love.

I would like to invite you to reflect personally and in community:

Questions for Personal Reflection:
1. What spiritual gifts have you identified in your life so far?

2. How are you using these gifts to build up the Church and serve others?

3. Do you feel like you're allowing the Holy Spirit to guide your service, or are you relying more on your own abilities?

4. How might you avoid falling into the trap of pride or rivalry in the use of your gifts?

Questions for Community Discernment:
1. Is our faith community equitably promoting the use of spiritual gifts?

2. What strategies could we implement to help new believers discover and apply their gifts?

3. Are we more focused on organizational structures or allowing the Holy Spirit to work freely in the midst of the body of Christ?

Dear reader, as you embark on this journey of discovery and action, remember that the Church is, at its core, a body in motion—alive, vibrant, and full of hope. Every gift, every talent, every capacity deposited by the Spirit is a sacred gift destined to strengthen unity and to advance God's global mission. How can you, in your personal journey, make your gifts shine for the glory of God and the growth of His Church? The invitation is clear: be an active co-worker and let the Spirit flow through you.

May this reflection inspire you to serve with love and to be an essential part of this wonderful body in motion. God bless you on your spiritual journey!

The Human Body Analogy: Unity and Diversity in the Church

Imagine for a moment that the Church is like a beautiful human body, where every cell, every organ, plays a vital role in keeping life in harmony. I myself have felt how, as a member of the body of Christ, my contribution has a meaning that transcends the individual and joins with others to form a united and vibrant organism. Paul reminds us in 1 Corinthians 12:12 that "for as the body is one, and has many members, but all the members of the body, being many, are one body, so also is Christ." This image inspires me to value both my gifts and those of others, knowing that no member is expendable for the mission God has entrusted to us.

From my personal experience, I have learned that sometimes we fall into the danger of thinking that we can live independently, without needing the other. Spiritual self-sufficiency is but an illusion that Paul piously overturns when he says, "And the eye cannot say unto the hand, I have no need of thee: nor again the head to the feet, I have no need of you" (1 Corinthians 12:21). I have seen in my own walk that when we stop supporting each other, communion is weakened and, as in a body, if an organ is missing, the total functioning is compromised.

I have also experienced how we can fall into the trap of exalting a part over the whole. Believing that only one gift or one function is more important generates division and pride, forgetting that diversity enriches our community life. And even more subtle is the contempt for those less visible gifts. Perhaps, at times, no one notices the silent intercession, the selfless hospitality, or the humble service; However, let us remember that "Nay, much more those members of the body, which seem to be more feeble, are necessary" (1 Corinthians 12:22). I have been blessed to see how, in the simple gift of a brother in hospitality or in the devotion of an intercessory team, the Spirit works mightily in building up the body of Christ.

The Latter Rain: Unleashing the Gifts for the End Time!

The Bible gives us inspiring examples that illustrate this diversity and unity. Consider the builders of the Tabernacle, Bezalel and Oholiab (Exodus 35:30-35), who were gifted with artistic skills to accomplish a sacred work; or the deacons of the early Church (Acts 6:1-7), chosen to steward resources and care for those in need. Even the teamwork of Paul and his co-workers, mentioned in Romans 16 (living shades of teachers, servants, and leaders), demonstrates that each role, however diverse it may seem, is indispensable to carrying out God's mission.

Christ is the Head and the very foundation of the Church. Ephesians 1:22 and Colossians 1:18 remind us that He leads and sustains everything. Through baptism, we are incorporated into the spiritual body: "For by one Spirit are we all baptized into one body, whether we be Jews or Gentiles, whether we be bond or free; and have been all made to drink into one Spirit" (1 Corinthians 12:13).

In the context of the Greco-Roman world, the head represented the center of thought and authority; in our Church, calling Christ "Head" highlights His absolute leadership, reminding us that without Him, unity and integral functioning are threatened. Today, although we face challenges such as excessive centralization of leadership, spiritual disconnection, or doctrinal fragmentation, the truth that we are one body in Christ impels us to seek unity and equity in service.

The wise Ellen G. White in the book The Great Controversy, she elaborated on this analogy, emphasizing that the Church of Christ, though composed of many members, must be a united body, working in harmony for the glory of God.

She also stated in Step to Christ, that separated from Christ, the members of the Church cannot fulfill their mission. Only in Him do we find the true source of power and direction. These words have constantly reminded me of the importance of depending on Christ in every aspect of my ministry and of fostering genuine interdependence in my community.

To invite you to reflect on your journey, I propose some questions that can help you discern and strengthen your commitment to the unity of the body of Christ:

Questions for Personal Reflection:
How can I contribute to the unity of the body of Christ in my life and ministry?

Do I recognize the importance of less visible gifts, such as intercession and hospitality?

Am I allowing Christ to truly be the Head of my life and service, or am I relying too much on my own strength?

What attitudes should I cultivate to avoid self-reliance and foster interdependence in faith?

Questions for Community Discernment:

Does our faith community promote the equal participation of all members? How can we help believers discover and use their gifts for the edification of the body?

Are we supporting the work of the Holy Spirit rather than emphasizing rigid organizational structures?

Dear friend, this study reminds us that the Church is a living organism, guided by the Holy Spirit and strengthened by the diversity of gifts God has bestowed. Each of us has a fundamental role in this body. My invitation is clear: let us commit ourselves to using our gifts for the glory of God and for the growth of His Church, for in that union and service, Christ's mission becomes a reality. How can you make sure today that your gift shines in perfect harmony with the rest of your body? May this reflection inspire you to live an active, interdependent and vibrant faith in the love of Christ.

Gifts for an Urgent Mission

From the beginning I understood that the Church is not simply a building or a motionless structure: it is a living body, in movement, in which each of us fulfills a vital function. In my walk with Christ, I have learned that, just as our body requires the coordination of its organs to beat, the Church operates in perfect harmony when each member heeds his or her spiritual calling. The Word reminds us in 1 Corinthians 12:12: "For as the body is one, and hath many members, and all the members of that one body, being many, are one body: so also is Christ."

This image moves me and challenges me to recognize that the gifts God places in each of us are not mere ornaments or general abilities, but concrete manifestations of divine grace meant to build up His people and to bring the light of His truth to where darkness is found.

Gifts for an Urgent Mission

Jesus, in his infinite compassion and vision, did not leave the Church without direction or power. In his promise he revealed to us the secret of mission fulfillment:

" But ye shall receive power, after that the Holy Ghost is come upon you: and ye shall be witnesses unto me both in Jerusalem, and in all Judaea, and in Samaria, and unto the uttermost part of the earth." (Acts 1:8).

This power of attorney is not generic; It is manifested through the multiplicity of spiritual gifts. Each of them—teaching, intercession, hospitality, prophecy, administration, faith, healing—has a very precise missionary function: to proclaim the virtues of the One who called us out of darkness into His marvelous light (1 Peter 2:9). In my life I have seen how, by putting these gifts into action, the Church ceases to be merely an observer of the events of the world and becomes a protagonist of the last great movement of redemption.

Imagine that a revival begins in secret, in the heart of every believer willing to let the Spirit work in him; an outpouring, known in Scripture as the "latter rain," will soon break out. Just as in ancient Israel's agriculture the latter rain ripened crops for the final harvest, the Spirit will enable the Church for a foreboding transformation. Today, when culture hijacks faith through secularization and indifference, we must fervently seek that outpouring that renews our missionary commitment.

The Mission of the Church and Spiritual Gifts

Spiritual gifts are not mere personal privileges; They are foundational tools for the mission of the gospel. Paul teaches us that every gift is given "for profit" (1 Corinthians 12:7), that is, for the building up of the body of Christ and for spreading the gospel in every corner of the world. I am reminded of the teachings of Jesus, whose preaching transformed lives by the authority that emanated from His word (Matthew 7:28-29), or how Moses, through the power of intercession, avoided divine judgments (Exodus 32:11-14). I also think of Lydia, whose gift of hospitality turned her home into a center of evangelization (Acts 16:14-15), and of Agabus, whose prophecy enabled the Church to prepare for moments of crisis (Acts 11:27-30).

These stories remind me that God endows each of us with specific capacities—whether they are to teach, intercede, welcome, or prophesy—for the sole purpose of proclaiming the victory of the Kingdom of God.

The Latter Rain and the Power of the Holy Spirit

The metaphor of "rain" in God's Word has been revealed to us as a symbol of the outpouring of the Holy Spirit. In ancient times, early rain began growth and late rain completed the maturation of crops. This was the case at Pentecost (Acts 2), when the first rain filled the Church with power, and promises that a second, more abundant rain will come before the second coming of Christ (Joel 2:23).

Today, many face secularization, spiritual indifference, and doctrinal fragmentation—challenges that urgently require a renewed outpouring of the Spirit. As soon as these gifts are manifested, we will see miracles, healings, mass conversions, and a vibrant witness that proclaims the glory of the One who transformed our darkness into light.

Ellen G. White and the Mission of the Gifts

Ellen White, recognized for her profound spiritual insight, emphasized that gifts are essential to the mission of the Church. She said that when the members of the Church are fully consecrated to the work of God, the Holy Ghost will be poured out in abundant measure, and the work of God will go forward with power.

He also reminded us of the importance of preparing our hearts in prayer and faith, because the latter rain will come upon those who, through faith and prayer, have prepared their hearts to receive it.

These words resonate in my heart every day, reminding me not to settle for passivity, but to give every gift for the glory of God and the expansion of the Kingdom.

Reflection and Discernment

In this call to an urgent mission, I invite you to meditate on some questions that can guide you on your journey:

Questions for Personal Reflection:
- How can you use your spiritual gifts for the mission of the Church in your daily life?

- Are you actively seeking the outpouring of the Holy Spirit in your life?

- What steps can you take today to prepare for the impending rain of a global revival?

- What personal obstacles might you be facing that prevent the Spirit from working with power in you?

Questions for Community Discernment:
- Is our Church focused on mission or has it been distracted by secondary issues?

- What concrete actions can we take to foster a greater commitment to evangelization and service?

- Are we praying and working together to receive that latter rain that will transform our communities?

- How can we help each believer discover and apply his or her spiritual gifts?

Dear brother or sister, each of us is vital to fulfilling Christ's mission. The Church can never reach its full potential without the power of the Holy Spirit working through us. I invite you to open yourself to that power, to use your gift to illuminate the darkness, and to become an active witness to God's transforming grace. Are you ready to be a part of this great movement of redemption?

May the Lord bless and guide you every step of this exciting and urgent journey toward the full manifestation of His Kingdom.

The Latter Rain: Unleashing the Gifts for the End Time!

Chapter 2: About Spiritual Gifts

A few years ago, as I meditated on God's Word, I understood that talking about spiritual gifts is not the same as talking about human abilities or inherited talents. It is to step into sacred ground, into the very language of the Spirit, into the way God equips His people for the greatest work in the universe — to be His ambassadors on earth. As I remember the words of 1 Corinthians 12:7, "But the manifestation of the Spirit is given to every man to profit withal." I realize that these gifts are not personal privileges. they are divine tools intended for the building up of the Church and the spread of the gospel, powerful demonstrations of God's power at work in the life of every believer.

One of the keys to understanding these heavenly gifts lies in the etymology of the term "spiritual gifts." The word comes from two fundamental Greek terms. On the one hand, **charismata (χαρίσματα),** which means "gifts of grace," reminds us that these gifts are bestowed by God without our being able to merit them by our own efforts. On the other hand, we find **pneumatikon (πνευματικόν),** translated as "the things of the Spirit", emphasizing that these are manifestations of the Holy Spirit. This truth fills me with wonder because it teaches me that our gifts are not earned; are received, being offered from heaven to edify His people.

The Latter Rain: Unleashing the Gifts for the End Time!

The Bible shows us, throughout Scripture, how these gifts have been put into action. I think of the gift of wisdom God bestowed upon Solomon (1 Kings 3:9-12), enabling him to rule justly; or Isaiah, who received the gift of prophecy to proclaim God's message to Israel (Isaiah 6:8-9). I am also reminded of the gift of healing in Peter, in healing a lame man at the door of the temple (Acts 3:6-8), and the gift of teaching in Paul, who spent years instructing believers in Ephesus (Acts 19:8-10). Each of these gifts was given for a single purpose: to edify, guide, and strengthen God's people. When I meditate on these examples, I feel that God calls us to actively participate in His ministry, using what He has entrusted to us to impact lives.

In ancient times, in the Greco-Roman world, gifts were seen as natural abilities or talents acquired through training. However, biblical teaching breaks with that perspective by showing us that spiritual gifts are supernatural manifestations, divine gifts from the Holy Spirit. Today, we face similar challenges: modern society tends to highlight human talent over the work of the Spirit, many fall into individualism believing that gifts are personal tools rather than instruments for collective edification, and are often mistaken for natural abilities, thus losing the miraculous and supernatural dimension of God's grace.

In my own spiritual journey, Ellen G. White's words have been a source of inspiration. She reminds us in

The Latter Rain: Unleashing the Gifts for the End Time!

The Great Controversy that "God has endowed His Church with various talents, and each one is to be employed for His glory. The work of God is not advanced by the efforts of a few, but by the cooperation of all.

Likewise, she said, the true success in the work of God does not depend on human eloquence, but on the presence of the Holy Spirit in every effort.

These statements teach me to depend completely on the Holy Spirit, to recognize that every gift, no matter how great or small it may seem, has a fundamental role in the body of Christ.

I invite you, then, to reflect and discern in your life:

Questions for Personal Reflection:

1. Have you identified the spiritual gifts God has given you?

2. How can you use these gifts to build up the Church and spread the gospel?

3. Are you allowing the Holy Ghost to guide your service, or are you relying more on your own abilities?

4. What attitudes do you need to cultivate to avoid falling into pride or competition for your gifts?

Questions for Community Discernment:

1. Is our Church promoting the equitable use of spiritual gifts among its members?

2. In what ways can we help new believers discover and exercise their gifts?

3. Are we prioritizing the transforming work of the Holy Spirit over merely human organizational structures?

This meditation reminds me every day that spiritual gifts are manifestations of the Holy Spirit given for the edification of the Church and for bringing the gospel message to the world. Every believer, without exception, has a vital role in this living body. How can you make your gift shine today for the glory of God and for the growth of his Church? May you find in this call the inspiration to move forward in your spiritual journey, knowing that you are part of a divine purpose that transcends your own existence.

What Spiritual Gifts Are Not

Throughout my journey in faith, I have discovered that spiritual gifts are not merely human abilities, inherited talents, or hard-won virtues. To speak of them is to enter sacred territory, in the very language of the Spirit, in the way God equips His people to accomplish the greatest work in history —

to be His ambassadors on earth. I am reminded of the inspiring words of 1 Corinthians 12:7, which assure us: "But to each one is given the manifestation of the Spirit for profit."

This manifestation is not a personal privilege, but a divine tool given to build up the Church and spread the gospel. However, over time many confusions have been brewing about what spiritual gifts are and, above all, what they are not. Let me share with you some truths that I have discovered in my journey:

1. **The gift of the Spirit is the living presence of the Holy Spirit in the believer, the foundation on which everything else is built.**

    Jesus promises us in John 14:16-17: " And I will pray the Father, and he shall give you another Comforter, that he may abide with you for ever; Even the Spirit of truth; whom the world cannot receive, because it seeth him not, neither knoweth him: but ye know him; for he dwelleth with you, and shall be in you."

2. **They are not natural talents.** Talents can be inherited or developed, and both believers and unbelievers can possess them. In contrast, spiritual gifts are bestowed only on those who have been born of Christ, as Paul teaches in Romans 12:6:

"Having then gifts differing according to the grace that is given to us, whether prophecy, let us prophesy according to the proportion of faith."

3. **They are not the fruit of the Spirit.** While the fruit of the Spirit describes the character of Christ formed in us—love, joy, peace, among others—spiritual gifts are meant to describe the service we render to others. Galatians 5:22-23 reminds us of the inner transformation that the Spirit works:

"But the fruit of the Spirit is love, joy, peace, longsuffering, gentleness, goodness, faith, Meekness, temperance: against such there is no law."

4. **They are not offices or positions.** Although a gift can support a trade, not everyone who holds a trade necessarily possesses the corresponding gift, nor vice versa.

5. **These are not general responsibilities.** It is true that we are all called to pray, to give, and to testify, but there are those who have been given a special gift to do so with extraordinary power.

6. **They are not imitations or fakes.** It is necessary to discern because Satan can also imitate signs; but, unlike Him, nothing can reproduce the fruit

of the Spirit or generate true edification in the Church. Jesus warns in Matthew 7:22-23:

"Many will say to me in that day, Lord, Lord, have we not prophesied in thy name? and in thy name have cast out devils? and in thy name done many wonderful works? And then will I profess unto them, I never knew you: depart from me, ye that work iniquity."

The Bible gives us clear examples of how to differentiate the genuine from the imitated. I am reminded of the case of Simon Magus in Acts 8:9-24, who attempted to purchase the power of the Spirit, being rebuked by Peter. Or the reign of Saul, who, though he had human authority, lacked the true presence of the Spirit (1 Samuel 16:14). Even during times of false prophets in Jeremiah's day (Jeremiah 23:16-17), the importance of discerning what comes from God from what is mere imitation was evident.

In the context of the ancient world, gifts were considered natural abilities or acquired through training. Biblical revelation, however, teaches us that spiritual gifts are supernatural manifestations, gifts offered from heaven. Today, we face similar challenges:

- The **confusion between talent and gift**, as many believe that these gifts are simply human abilities.

- The appearance of **false miracles and signs** that, while they may seem impressive, lack genuine inner transformation.

- The **lack of discernment**, necessary to distinguish what comes from the Holy Spirit from what is mere imitation.

In this sense, Ellen White's words have illuminated my path. She wisely stated in *The Great Controversy*: that the enemy will try to imitate the gifts of the Spirit, but true gifts will always lead to obedience and the edification of God's people.

She also reminded us in *Step to Crist*, of the importance of discernment, that not everything that seems miraculous comes from God. We must test the spirits to see if they are of God.

These truths have helped me develop a deeper discernment, to ensure that every gift that is manifested in my life or in the community is genuine and meant for the glory of God.

I invite you to reflect personally and in community:

Questions for Personal Reflection:
1. Have you ever confused a natural talent with a spiritual gift?

2. How can you make sure you're using your gifts for God's glory, rather than for your own benefit?

3. Have you observed or experienced signs or miracles that, despite their appearance, did not produce true edification in the community?

4. What steps can you take to develop deeper spiritual insight that allows you to identify the true gifts of the Spirit?

Questions for Community Discernment:

1. Is our Church promoting a clear and honest understanding of spiritual gifts?

2. How can we help believers distinguish between talents, fruits, and gifts?

3. Are we warning the community about the danger of false signs and miracles?

4. How can we foster a greater reliance on the Holy Ghost in discerning these gifts?

In the end, I remember that spiritual gifts are manifestations of the Holy Spirit, not mere human abilities or mere empty signs. Every believer has a fundamental role in the body of Christ, and only by using them for the glory of God and for the building up of the Church, can we fulfill the mission entrusted to us. How do you ensure that your gifts are used for the growth and glory of the Kingdom? May this reflection spur you to cultivate deep discernment and to serve with total dependence on the Holy Spirit.

Definition and Characteristics of Spiritual Gifts

A spiritual gift is a supernatural ability given by the Holy Spirit to every believer to build up the body of Christ and fulfill the mission of the Kingdom. These gifts are:

1. **Bestowed by grace** – Not received by human merit, but by God's will.

2. Distributed by the Spirit according to His will – "Many will say to me in that day, Lord, Lord, have we not prophesied in thy name? and in thy name have cast out devils? and in thy name done many wonderful works? And then will I profess unto them, I never knew you: depart from me, ye that work iniquity." (1 Corinthians 12:11).

3. Given to serve others, not to exalt oneself – "As every man hath received the gift, even so minister the same one to another, as good stewards of the manifold grace of God." (1 Peter 4:10).

4. Diverse, but operating in unity – " There is one body, and one Spirit, even as ye are called in one hope of your calling; One Lord, one faith, one baptism, One God and Father of all, who is above all, and through all, and in you all. But unto every one of us is given grace according to the measure of the gift of Christ" (Ephesians 4:4-7).

5. Effective only when exercised with love. "Though I speak with the tongues of men and of angels, and have not charity, I am become as sounding brass, or a tinkling cymbal" (1 Corinthians 13:1).

Discovering and Activating Spiritual Gifts: A Call to Transformation

Paul reminds us that **every Christian has received at least one spiritual gift**, a manifestation of the Holy Spirit meant to glorify God and build up His Church. However, it **is not enough to possess a gift; it is our responsibility to discover it, activate it, and use it with purpose.**

This process is not a guessing game or a matter of luck. **It is a journey of prayer, discernment, humility, and action.** It is opening up to the Holy Spirit and telling Him sincerely, "*Here I am, use me as You will.*"

When the gifts are activated, **the Church will be transformed.** Fire will run through dry bones, testimony will be powerful, and heaven will move in response to a Church operating under the power of the Spirit.

Biblical Examples of Gift Discovery

Throughout biblical history, we see how God has called and equipped His servants with specific gifts to fulfill His purpose.

- **Moses and Leadership (Exodus 3:10-12):** Although he doubted his ability, God called him and equipped him to lead His people.

- **Samuel and prophetic discernment (1 Samuel 3:1-10):** He learned to listen to God's voice and respond with obedience.

- **Paul and the gift of teaching (Acts 9:15-20):** He was transformed by the power of Christ and sent to preach with authority.

Each of them had **to discover their calling, trust in God's direction, and exercise their gift courageously.**

Today, the same Spirit who empowered Moses, Samuel, and Paul **is at work in us, calling us to discover and activate the gifts we have been given.**

The Historical and Cultural Context of Spiritual Gifts

In the ancient world, gifts were seen as natural abilities or acquired by training. **Biblical teaching breaks with this idea by affirming that spiritual**

gifts are supernatural manifestations of the Holy Spirit.

Today, the Church faces similar challenges:

- **Confusion between talent and gift:** Many believe that spiritual gifts are simply human abilities, when in fact they are divine impartations.

- **Lack of discernment:** The Church must learn to distinguish between what comes from the Spirit and what is imitation or manipulation.

- **Disconnection from mission:** Some believers do not use their gifts for the edification of the body of Christ, but for personal ends or for the satisfaction of the audience.

If we want to see a Church vibrant and filled with God's power, **we must recover the true teaching on spiritual gifts and align ourselves with the will of the Holy Spirit.**

Ellen G. White emphasized that **spiritual gifts are essential to the mission of the Church.** In The Great Controversy, he said that when the members of the Church are fully consecrated to the work of God, the Holy Ghost will be poured out in abundant measure, and the work of God will go forward with power.

The Latter Rain: Unleashing the Gifts for the End Time!

This message is more relevant than ever. **The activation of the gifts is not a luxury, but an urgent necessity for the advancement of the Kingdom.**

He also highlighted the importance of love in the exercise of gifts: White say that true success in the work of God does not depend on human eloquence, but on the presence of the Holy Spirit in every effort.

It's not about how talented we are, or how well we can speak, teach, or serve. **It's about how much we allow the Holy Spirit to flow through us.**

A Call to Action

If every believer discovered and activated his spiritual gift, the Church would experience unprecedented revival.

The Holy Spirit has already deposited a gift in you. Now it is your responsibility to seek it out, develop it, and use it for the glory of God.

Don't let fear, doubt, or complacency keep you from walking in your calling. Pray, study, serve, and allow the Holy Spirit to guide you in this process.

When the gifts are activated, the Church will be strengthened, the world will see God's power in action, and the Kingdom will move forward with authority.

The Latter Rain: Unleashing the Gifts for the End Time!

It's time to wake up. It is time to discover and activate your gift.

May the Holy Ghost guide you on this journey and may your life be a living testimony of His power!

Reflection and Discernment
Questions for Personal Reflection

1. Have you identified the spiritual gifts God has given you?

2. How can you use your gifts for the edification of the Church and the spread of the gospel?

3. Are you allowing the Holy Spirit to guide your service, or are you leaning more on your own abilities?

4. How can you avoid pride or competition in the use of spiritual gifts?

Questions for Community Discernment
1. Is our Church promoting the use of spiritual gifts in an equitable manner?

2. How can we help new believers discover their gifts and put them into practice?

3. Are we focusing more on organizational structures than on the work of the Holy Spirit?

This study reminds us that spiritual gifts are **manifestations of the Holy Spirit**, not human talents or empty signs. Every believer has a fundamental role in the body of Christ. How can we make sure we are using our gifts for the glory of God and the growth of His Church? Throughout my walk with Christ, I have come to understand that spiritual gifts are not mere human abilities, inherited talents, or hard-earned behaviors.

They are, instead, supernatural gifts bestowed by the Holy Spirit on every believer, designed to build up the body of Christ and to fulfill the mission of the Kingdom.

This truth is reflected in 1 Corinthians 12:7, where we are told: "But the manifestation of the Spirit is given to every man to profit withal.

I have learned that these gifts have very specific characteristics:

1. **Granted by grace.** They are not earned by human merit, but are the result of God's sovereign will.

2. Distributed by the Spirit according to His will. As 1 Corinthians 12:11 reminds us: "But all these worketh that one and the selfsame Spirit, dividing to every man severally as he will." This indicates that the assignment of each gift is unique and perfect in its purpose.

3. Given to serve others, not to exalt oneself. In 1 Peter 4:10 we are invited to exercise our gifts as good stewards of God's manifold grace, reminding us that our service should always reflect Christ's selfless love.

4. Ephesians 4:4-7 teaches us that, although we are many and our gifts varied, we are all part of one body, called in one hope.

5. Effective only when exercised with love. This is how Paul expressed it in 1 Corinthians 13:1, warning us that without love, even the most impressive gifts are like a cymbal that tinkles without producing fruit.

Paul goes on to emphasize that every Christian possesses at least one gift, and the responsibility we have is to identify it and put it at the service of God and the body of Christ.

In my experience, discovering the spiritual gift is not a guessing game, but a profound journey of prayer, discernment, humility, and action. It is that moment when, in silence and in communion, we open ourselves to the Spirit and say: "Here I am, use me as You will." As I look throughout Scripture, I find inspiring examples:

- **Moses**, called and empowered by God to lead Israel (Exodus 3:10-12), despite his doubts.

- **Samuel**, who learned to listen to God's voice in the intimacy of his youth (1 Samuel 3:1-10).

- **Paul**, radically transformed and sent to preach with authority (Acts 9:15-20).

Each of these examples encourages me to believe that, when our gifts are activated, the Church is transformed in amazing ways. The fire of the Spirit runs through the dry bones, the testimonies become powerful, and the sky seems to move.

It is important to remember that, in the Greco-Roman world, gifts were understood as natural abilities or skills acquired through training. Biblical teaching, however, reveals to us a radical truth: spiritual gifts are supernatural manifestations of the Holy Spirit. Today, the Church continues to face similar challenges, such as the confusion between talent and gift, the lack of discernment to distinguish what really comes from the Spirit, and the disconnection with divine mission.

In this context, Ellen White's words have been a light to me. In *The Great Controversy* she reminds us that when the members of the Church are fully consecrated to the work of God, the Holy Ghost will be poured out in abundant measure, and the work of God will go forward with power.

And in *Step to Christ* we can be reminded that the true success in the work of God does not depend on human eloquence, but on the presence of the Holy Spirit in every effort.

These teachings impel me to always seek the guidance of the Spirit, to cultivate my gifts and to exercise them with humility and love, remembering that the ultimate goal is the building up of the Church and the spread of the Gospel.

I invite you to reflect and discern in your own life:

Questions for Personal Reflection:

1. Have you identified the spiritual gifts God has given you?

2. How can you use them for the building up of the Church and for the spread of the gospel?

3. Do you allow the Holy Ghost to direct your service, or do you rely more on your own abilities?

4. What can you do to avoid pride or competition in the use of your gifts?

Questions for Community Discernment:

1. Is our Church promoting the equitable use of spiritual gifts?

2. How can we help new believers discover and apply their gifts?

3. Are we focused on allowing the Holy Spirit to work, rather than relying on, merely human organizational structures?

In conclusion, this study reminds me that spiritual gifts are true manifestations of the Holy Spirit, not mere human abilities or empty signs. Every believer, without exception, has a fundamental role in the body of Christ. How can we make sure we are using our gifts for the glory of God and for the growth of His Church? May this reflection inspire you to live in total dependence on the Spirit, serving with humility and transforming your environment in the light of the Gospel.

Chapter 3: The Distribution of the Gifts

Ever since I discovered the wonderful design of spiritual gifts, I have felt our faith transformed into something alive, dynamic, and deeply coordinated by the Holy Spirit. It is no accident that the Spirit does not act in arbitrary or chaotic ways; in His infinite wisdom and sovereignty, He doles out spiritual gifts with perfect order, divine purpose, and eternal vision. Understanding how these heavenly gifts are distributed has allowed me to see the harmony with which God has equipped His Church to fulfill His mission on earth.

I remember clearly what Paul says in 1 Corinthians 12:11: "But all these worketh that one and the selfsame Spirit, dividing to every man severally as he will."

This verse emphasizes that spiritual gifts are not chosen by us, but sovereignly bestowed by the Holy Spirit according to His will. Each believer receives a specific gift, designed for the edification of the body of Christ and the fulfillment of the divine mission.

If you want to delve deeper into the context of spiritual gifts, I recommend reading the entire 1 Corinthians 12, where Paul explains the diversity of gifts and their purpose within the Church.

This simple but powerful statement reminds me that, before us, it is the Spirit who decides what gift each believer receives. It is not a matter for us to choose, but God, in His perfect sovereignty, allocates each gift according to His purpose. It is comforting to imagine that every ability we see in our community is part of a divine plan, designed so that diversity—though seemingly dissimilar—becomes a perfect unity within the body of Christ.

The Bible teaches us several essential principles about the distribution of spiritual gifts. First, God is the one who decides what gift each believer receives.

As 1 Corinthians 12:7 says: "But the manifestation of the Spirit is given to every man to profit withal." Thus, it is not we who create these gifts, but they are the fruit of divine grace.

In addition, the gifts are incredibly diverse, but they function in complete unity. Paul teaches us in Romans 12:4: "For as we have many members in one body, and all members have not the same office:" I am convinced that this diversity reflects the richness and complexity of the body of Christ, where each member has a specific role to play.

Spiritual gifts are also given for the edification of the Church. In Ephesians 4:12 we are reminded: "For the perfecting of the saints, for the work of the ministry, for the edifying of the body of Christ."

They are not instruments for personal gain, but tools to strengthen and build our community of faith.

Finally, I have learned that these gifts only bear fruit when they are exercised in love. In 1 Corinthians 13:1, Paul warns us: " Though I speak with the tongues of men and of angels, and have not charity, I am become as sounding brass, or a tinkling cymbal." Without love, every action becomes empty, and our gifts lose their purpose and efficacy.

Biblical practice shows us how God distributed gifts to specific people to fulfill His purposes. I remember how Moses was called to lead Israel (Exodus 3:10-12), or how Bezalel and Oholiab were given the artistic ability to build the tabernacle (Exodus 31:1-6). I am also mindful of the powerful gift of preaching that Peter displayed on the day of Pentecost (Acts 2:14-41) and the gift of teaching that Paul used to form the Church doctrinally (Romans 1:1; 1 Timothy 2:7). Each of these examples inspires me to see that there are no small or insignificant gifts, but gifts that, for each specific task, have been uniquely entrusted to us by God.

In a historical context in which, in the Greco-Roman world, gifts were considered as acquired or natural skills, biblical teaching revolutionized that view. Today, in our society, we still face the challenge of confusing human talent with spiritual gift. Many may think that these gifts are simply natural skills; however, the reality is that they are supernatural manifestations of the Spirit. In addition, the lack of discernment as to what comes from God and what does not, or the disconnect between the use of gifts and the mission of the Church, remain challenges that we must overcome.

In moments of reflection, I find great wisdom in Ellen White's words. In *The Great Controversy* she wrote:

God has endowed His Church with diverse talents, and each one is to be employed for His glory. The work of God is not advanced by the efforts of a few, but by the cooperation of all.

And in *Step to Christ*, she emphasized that the true success in God's work does not depend on human eloquence, but on the presence of the Holy Spirit in every effort.

These truths constantly invite me to examine my dependence on the Holy Ghost and to make sure that my gift is used to build up the Church and not for my own exaltation.

I invite you, dear reader, to meditate on these questions and to sincerely seek discernment in your life:

The Latter Rain: Unleashing the Gifts for the End Time!

Questions for Personal Reflection:

1. Have you identified the spiritual gifts God has given you?

2. How can you use them for the building up of the Church and the spread of the gospel?

3. Do you allow the Holy Spirit to guide your service, or do you rely more on your own abilities?

4. What steps can you take to avoid pride or competition in the exercise of your gifts?

Questions for Community Discernment:

1. Does our Church promote the equitable use of spiritual gifts?

2. How can we help new believers discover and exercise their gifts?

3. Are we more focused on allowing the Holy Spirit to work or maintaining rigid organizational structures?

This meditation reminds me powerfully that spiritual gifts are true manifestations of the Holy Spirit, heavenly gifts meant for the edification of the body of Christ. Every believer has a fundamental role in this great mission. How can you ensure that your gifts are used for the glory of God and the growth of His Church? May this reflection inspire you to live in total dependence on the Spirit, serving humbly and passionately to shine the light of Christ in the world.

The Gifts and the Trinity

When I meditate on God's wonderful plan, I marvel to see that all of Deity is involved in the process of giving spiritual gifts. It is not an impulsive or chaotic act, but a perfect work of the Trinity, in which the Father, Son, and Holy Spirit work in complete harmony. As the apostle Paul reveals to us in 1 Corinthians 12:4-6:

"Now there are diversities of gifts, but the same Spirit. And there are differences of administrations, but the same Lord. And there are diversities of operations, but it is the same God which worketh all in all."

This statement fills me with amazement, for I know that it is not a human invention or merely a product of emotions; it is a sacred work whose divine origin goes back to the very heart of God.

The Participation of the Trinity in the Spiritual Gifts

In my walk with Christ, I have learned to recognize the wonderful work of the **Trinity** in the distribution and functioning of spiritual gifts. Each divine person—the Father, Son, and Holy Spirit—has an essential role in this process, ensuring that each gift is imparted with purpose and precision.

God the Father: The Source of All Gift

Every spiritual gift has its origin in God the Father, who, in His sovereignty, grants them for a divine purpose. There is no skill, talent, or spiritual manifestation that does not come from His generous hand.

James 1:17 reminds us of this truth: " Every good gift and every perfect gift is from above, and cometh down from the Father of lights, with whom is no variableness, neither shadow of turning."

As I reflect on this verse, I am filled with gratitude to know that every gift we receive is a perfect gift, designed by the Father to fulfill His will in our lives and in His Church.

Jesus Christ: The Lord of Ministries

Jesus, our Savior and Master, not only redeemed us, but He also established the ministries within His Church. Through His example and authority, He assigns specific roles for the building up of the body of Christ.

The Latter Rain: Unleashing the Gifts for the End Time!

Ephesians 4:11 tells us, "And he himself appointed some apostles; others, prophets; others, evangelists; others, pastors and teachers."

Every ministry has a unique purpose, and Jesus is the one who calls and empowers His servants to fulfill the mission He has designed. When I think about this, I realize that we don't choose our calling by personal preference; it is Christ who assigns us according to His will.

The Holy Spirit: The Distributor of the Gifts

Finally, it is the Holy Spirit who distributes spiritual gifts in intentional and personalized ways. He knows our abilities, our disposition, and where we will be most effective in the Kingdom of God.

1 Corinthians 12:11 states, "But all these things are done by one and the same Spirit, dividing to each one individually as he wills."

This verse reminds me that gifts are not assigned randomly, but with divine precision. The Holy Ghost, in His wisdom, equips us with what we need to fulfill our purpose in the Church and in the world.

Final Thoughts

When we understand the **Godhead**'s participation in spiritual gifts, **our service takes on a deeper meaning.** We are not operating in our own strength, but under the direction of the Father, Son, and Holy Spirit.

Every gift we receive is a reflection of the Father's love, Christ's authority, and the work of the Holy Spirit in us.

Are we willing to receive, develop, and use the gifts God has given us?

May this truth transform the way we serve, reminding us that we are instruments in the hands of a perfect God, called to build His Church and glorify His name.

May the Holy Spirit guide us on this beautiful journey of discovery and activation of our gifts!

Biblical Examples of the Trinity in Action

I have found in the Scriptures vibrant examples of this unity in the work of the Godhead. I am reminded of Jesus' baptism in Matthew 3:16-17, where the Father spoke, the Spirit descended, and the Son was confirmed in His mission. I am also moved by the Great Commission, when Jesus sent His disciples in the name of the Father, the Son, and the Holy Spirit (Matthew 28:19), and the powerful manifestation of Pentecost (Acts 2:1-4), where the Spirit empowered the early believers for a global mission. Each of these events is a testimony of the perfect unity and purpose of the Godhead in God's work.

Historical and Cultural Context

In the Greco-Roman world, the notion of a Trinity was alien to the prevailing philosophy. However, the early Church challenged these paradigms, proclaiming that God is one in essence but three in persons, and that each divine member actively participates in the salvation and building up of the Church. Today, our community faces very similar challenges:

- There is doctrinal confusion, as some downplay or even deny the importance of the Trinity.

- Spiritual individualism often causes each believer to see his or her gifts as personal tools, forgetting the interdependence that should characterize the Church.

- Lack of dependence on the Spirit leads us to emphasize human methods rather than allowing God's supernatural power to operate in our midst.

In my search for a deeper understanding, I have found great clarity in the work of Ellen White. She reminded us in *The Great Controversy* that when the Father, the Son, and the Holy Spirit are working together for the salvation of man and the building up of his Church. Every gift is an expression of his love and power.

Likewise, in *Step to Christ,* she emphasized that without the Holy Spirit, the gifts cannot operate effectively. It is divine power that transforms human talents into tools for the glory of God."

These words have strengthened me in my faith and encourage me to depend fully on the Holy Spirit, reminding me that our gifts flow from the love and power of the Trinity.

Reflection and Discernment
I invite you to join me in this reflection, asking you:

1. How can you recognize the work of the Godhead in your life and ministry?

2. Are you depending on the Holy Ghost as you exercise your spiritual gifts?

3. How can you make sure your gifts are in full harmony with God's will?

4. Have you noticed how spiritual gifts strengthen the unity of the Church in your community?

As for your community, you may be able to reflect with other believers:

1. Is our Church rightly teaching the doctrine of the Trinity?

2. How can we foster a greater reliance on the Holy Ghost in all our activities?

3. Are we effectively using spiritual gifts for the edification of the body of Christ?

4. How can we help believers discover and use their gifts so that everything flows to the glory of God?

This study constantly reminds me that spiritual gifts are manifestations of the Holy Ghost, bestowed by the Father and guided by the Son. Each of us has a critical role in the body of Christ. How can we make sure we are using these gifts for the glory of God and the growth of His Church? May this meditation inspire you to live in unity and dependence on the power of the Trinity, recognizing in each gift the sacred hand that grants it.

Who Receives Spiritual Gifts?

In my walk of faith, I have discovered that not everyone receives spiritual gifts—only those who are born again and belong to the body of Christ are the true recipients of these pleasing manifestations of the Spirit. The Word is clear in 1 Corinthians 12:7:

"But the manifestation of the Spirit is given to every man to profit withal."

And in 1 Peter 4:10 we are instructed, "As every man hath received the gift, even so minister the same one to another, as good stewards of the manifold grace of God."

This truth has taught me that spiritual gifts are not given to just anyone, but are confidential gifts intended for those who have been transformed by Christ. God is no respecter of persons; He distributes these gifts according to His will and with a very clear purpose: to build His Church and fulfill His mission on earth.

Throughout my life, I have meditated on the biblical principles that govern the reception of these gifts. First, only believers in Christ have the privilege of receiving them, for, as 1 Corinthians 12:13 says, "For by one Spirit are we all baptized into one body, whether we be Jews or Gentiles, whether we be bond or free; and have been all made to drink into one Spirit."

This intimate and sacred union sets us apart and enables us to serve in the Kingdom of God. Moreover, every believer, without exception, receives at least one gift, and it is the Spirit himself who distributes to each one "But all these worketh that one and the selfsame Spirit, dividing to every man severally as he will." (1 Corinthians 12:11).

The Latter Rain: Unleashing the Gifts for the End Time!

I have found living examples in the scriptures of how God bestows gifts on different individuals to fulfill His purpose. I remember with awe how Moses was called and equipped to lead Israel (Exodus 3:10-12), or how Bezalel and Oholiab were given the artistic skill needed to build the tabernacle (Exodus 31:1-6). Likewise, Peter's powerful preaching gift at Pentecost (Acts 2:14-41) and Paul's teaching gift (Romans 1:1; 1 Timothy 2:7) are testimony that, in God's plan, every task is assigned a special gift.

It is fascinating to think that, in the Greco-Roman context, gifts were understood simply as natural abilities or tools acquired by training. However, biblical revelation shows us that gifts are supernatural manifestations of the Holy Spirit. Today, the Church faces similar challenges, such as the confusion that exists between talent and gift, or the lack of discernment in distinguishing what comes from the Spirit and what is mere imitation. Furthermore, some believers may be tempted not to use their gifts for the building up of the body of Christ, reminding us of the importance of always maintaining connection to the transforming work of the Spirit.

In my personal meditation, Ellen White's teachings have been a beacon of clarity and righteousness. She wrote in *The Great Controversy* that when God has endowed His Church with diverse talents, and each one is to be employed for His glory. The work of

God is not advanced by the efforts of a few, but by the cooperation of all.

This reminds me that if I want my service to have a lasting impact, I must use my gift not for my own exaltation, but to contribute to the strength of the community. Similarly, in the *Steps to Christ*, emphasizes that true success in God's work does not depend on human eloquence, but on the presence of the Holy Spirit in every effort.

As I reflect on all of this, I invite myself to examine my heart and my service to God with some questions for personal reflection:
- Have I clearly identified the spiritual gifts God has given me?

- How can I best use them for the building up of the Church and the spread of the gospel?

- Am I allowing the Holy Ghost to guide my service, or am I overly reliant on my own abilities?

- What attitudes should I cultivate to avoid falling into pride or unnecessary competition?

It is also vital that, as a community, we ask ourselves:
- Does our Church promote the equitable use of spiritual gifts among its members?

- How can we make it easier for new believers to discover and apply their gifts?

- Are we focusing on the work of the Holy Spirit or on organizational structures that can sometimes hinder genuine divine movement?

This meditation on who receives spiritual gifts reminds me that every believer is invaluable to the body of Christ. In God's grace and fellowship, there is no one without the other, and we are all called to serve and to edify. How can you make sure today that you are using your gifts for the glory of God and for the growth of His Church? May this reflection inspire you to rediscover and share the unique gift that the Spirit has entrusted to you, so that together we can advance in the transforming mission of the Kingdom.

This study reminds us that spiritual gifts are **manifestations of the Holy Ghost**, bestowed by the Father and guided by the Son. Every believer has a fundamental role in the body of Christ. How can we make sure we are using our gifts for the glory of God and the growth of His Church?

When Are Spiritual Gifts Imparted?

In my spiritual walk I have come to deeply appreciate that spiritual gifts are imparted at the very moment we receive the Holy Spirit, when we experience the new birth in Christ. This transforming revelation became visible on the day of

The Latter Rain: Unleashing the Gifts for the End Time!

Pentecost, when "they were all filled with the Holy Spirit, and began to speak in other tongues, as the Spirit gave them utterance" (Acts 2:4). It was then that the gifts began to manifest themselves in the lives of the disciples, and with them the Church was enabled to fulfill her mission of transforming the world.

This moment of conversion marks not only a change in our inner life, but also the beginning of a legacy of service that extends throughout the history of the Church. Every genuine conversion is, in fact, an inauguration of gifts. The Holy Spirit comes to dwell in the believer not only to sanctify him, but also to enable him and use him in the work of God. As 1 Corinthians 12:13 says, "For by one Spirit are we all baptized into one body, whether we be Jews or Gentiles, whether we be bond or free; and have been all made to drink into one Spirit," which means that, from the moment we respond to grace, we are equipped with supernatural resources to serve and build up the Church.

The Bible clearly states several principles about when and how believers receive these precious gifts. First, we are taught that gifts are imparted the instant we receive the Holy Spirit, marking the beginning of a new life. Then, the Pentecost model shows us that this outpouring is not for personal gain, but for the witness and spread of the gospel, as Jesus declares in Acts 1:8: "But ye shall receive power, after that the Holy Ghost is come upon you:

and ye shall be witnesses unto me both in Jerusalem, and in all Judaea, and in Samaria, and unto the uttermost part of the earth."

In addition, every believer receives at least one gift "But the manifestation of the Spirit is given to every man to profit withal" (1 Corinthians 12:7), and while these gifts are imparted at the time of conversion, they can also be developed and perfected over time, as Paul exhorts us in 2 Timothy 1:6: "Wherefore I put thee in remembrance that thou stir up the gift of God, which is in thee by the putting on of my hands."

The predictive narrative of our faith is reflected in biblical examples that have guided me throughout my life. I remember the powerful experience of the disciples at Pentecost, when they were filled with the Spirit and began to manifest gifts in an evident way, radically transforming their way of living and preaching. Similarly, I think of Paul, who after his conversion on the road to Damascus (Acts 9:17-20) was filled with power and passion to proclaim the gospel, or Timothy, whose gift was confirmed through the laying on of hands (1 Timothy 4:14), in the context of a robust community of faith that supported him.

It is interesting to note how, in the Greco-Roman world, gifts were understood as natural or training-acquired abilities. However, our God breaks that limited vision by revealing to us that spiritual gifts are supernatural manifestations of the Holy Spirit. Today, we face similar challenges: there is much confusion between talent and gift, and often the Church must learn anew to distinguish what truly comes from the Spirit and what is imitation. In addition, there are those who, unfortunately, do not use their gifts for the building up of the body of Christ.

In this regard, White's words have been a light to my spirit. In *The Great Controversy* she reminds us that when the members of the Church are fully consecrated to the work of God, the Holy Ghost will be poured out in abundant measure, and the work of God will go forward with power.

And also, that without the Holy Spirit, the gifts cannot operate effectively. It is divine power that transforms human talents into tools for the glory of God.

These truths prompt me to examine my own life, to always seek the guidance of the Holy Ghost in my service, and to strive to cultivate and exercise the gift God has entrusted to me.

I encourage you to also reflect within yourself:

Questions for Personal Reflection
1. Have you identified the spiritual gifts God has given you since the time of your conversion?

2. How can you use these gifts for the building up of the Church and the spread of the gospel?

3. Do you allow the Holy Ghost to guide your service, or do you rely too much on your own abilities?

4. What concrete steps can you take to avoid pride or competition in the manifestation of your gifts?

Questions for Community Discernment

1. Is our Church equitably promoting the use of spiritual gifts among its members?

2. What actions can we implement to help new believers discover and exercise their gifts?

3. Are we focusing on allowing the power of the Holy Spirit to work in our midst, rather than relying exclusively on organizational structures?

This meditation reminds me that the moment we receive the Spirit is also the moment we are empowered to serve, and that our commitment to grow and put those gifts into practice is central to God's mission on earth. How can you, today, renew that self-giving and allow your gifts to be fully manifested in the service of the Kingdom? May this reflection inspire you to walk daily in the presence and power of the Holy Spirit, letting His work in you transform the world around you.

This study reminds us that spiritual gifts are **manifestations of the Holy Ghost**, bestowed by the Father and guided by the Son. Every believer has a fundamental role in the body of Christ. How can we make sure we are using our gifts for the glory of God and the growth of His Church?

Purpose of Spiritual Gifts
Throughout my journey of faith, I have learned that the purpose of spiritual gifts is clear and transformative: they are not given to us as personal trophies or as instruments of self-promotion, but as tools of service to build up the body of Christ and equip it for the work of ministry. I remember with gratitude when I was studying Ephesians 4:12, and I understood that these gifts exist " For the perfecting of the saints, for the work of the ministry, for the edifying of the body of Christ." This truth has prompted me to see in every gift of the Spirit an invitation to be an active part of God's mission.

In my experience, every gift is a manifestation of God's grace, given without human merit, to serve others and not to exalt the individual. This is stated by 1 Corinthians 12:7: "But the manifestation of the Spirit is given to every man to profit withal."

This purpose reminds us that gifts do not exist for our personal well-being, but to strengthen and enrich the community of faith. It is a reminder that we share the same calling in Christ—though each of us is different, in God's love we form one body.

Another critical aspect is that gifts enable us to do the work of ministry. Paul exhorts us in Romans 12:6, " Having then gifts differing according to the grace that is given to us, whether prophecy, let us prophesy according to the proportion of faith."

Each believer receives a spectacular gift, a unique resource that, when exercised, becomes a powerful tool for the expansion of the gospel and the strengthening of the Church.

The diversity of these gifts, so necessary for unity and spiritual growth—as we are reminded in Ephesians 4:4: " There is one body, and one Spirit, even as ye are called in one hope of your calling"—shows that the true strength of the Church lies in the interdependence of its members.

For me, it is especially inspiring to recognize that the purpose of each gift is manifested in practice. I think of Moses, who was called and equipped to lead Israel (Exodus 3:10-12); in Bezalel and Oholiab, who received the gift of craftsmanship to build the tabernacle (Exodus 31:1-6); in Peter, whose gift of preaching ignited thousands of souls at Pentecost (Acts 2:14-41); and in Paul, who through his teaching strengthened the Church doctrinally (Romans 1:1; 1 Timothy 2:7). Each of these biblical examples teaches me that, in God's plan, there are no insignificant gifts: they are all destined for a common purpose, which is to build up and strengthen God's people.

The Latter Rain: Unleashing the Gifts for the End Time!

In the historical and cultural context of the Greco-Roman world, gifts were often seen only as natural abilities or acquired skills. However, biblical teaching invites us to look further, to understand that spiritual gifts are supernatural manifestations of the Holy Spirit. Today, in our own community, we face similar challenges. Many still confuse human talent with the gift of the Spirit, and the lack of discernment forces us to distinguish carefully between what truly comes from God and what is simply the fruit of natural capacities. At times, some believers do not even use their gift to build up the body, but rather retain or misinterpret it, thus separating the gift from its original purpose.

In these respects, the teachings of Mrs. White have been a beacon in my spiritual journey. She always reminds me that when the members of the Church are fully consecrated to the work of God, the Holy Ghost will be poured out in abundant measure, and the work of God will go forward with power.

And she also exhorts us to work in unity, because when the members of the Church work in harmony, each using the gifts God has given him, the body of Christ is strengthened and the gospel advances with power.

These words challenge me day by day to let go of any inclination to pride or competition, reminding me that true success in God's work does not depend on eloquence or personal accomplishments, but on how our gifts serve to edify others.

I would like to invite you, dear friend, to reflect and search in your life for the following:

Questions for Personal Reflection:
1. Have you identified the spiritual gifts God has given you and understood their purpose for building you up?

2. How can you use these gifts to strengthen the Church and spread the gospel?

3. Do you rely on the Holy Ghost to guide your service, or do you rely heavily on your own abilities?

4. What concrete steps can you take to avoid pride and competition and serve with humility and love?

Questions for Community Discernment:
1. Is our Church promoting the use of spiritual gifts in an equitable manner?

2. How can we help new believers discover and apply their gifts?

3. Are we prioritizing the transforming work of the Holy Spirit over rigid organizational structures?

This meditation on the purpose of the gifts reminds me that, in the end, God has equipped us not to receive praise individually, but to work together and build His Church. Every gift is a divine gift meant to glorify God and to encourage the growth of a strong and united body of faith. How can you make sure today that your gift is used for the glory of God and for the well-being of His Church? May these reflections spur you to be an active witness and to serve with love, fulfilling the mission that God has placed in you.

This study reminds us that spiritual gifts are **manifestations of the Holy Ghost**, bestowed by the Father and guided by the Son. Every believer has a fundamental role in the body of Christ. How can we make sure we are using our gifts for the glory of God and the growth of His Church?

Duration of Spiritual Gifts
In my walk with Christ, I have learned that spiritual gifts are a permanent gift as long as we abide in Him. Although I have sometimes wondered if these gifts, which so powerfully equip us for the work of ministry, will fade in time, I have discovered in the Word that their essence is irrevocable. Paul assures us in Romans 11:29, " For the gifts and calling of God are without repentance."

This truth comforts me, knowing that as long as I maintain my fellowship with Christ, the Holy Spirit will continue to work in my life. However, I have also learned that gifts can develop or even atrophy according to our relationship with God. It is as if each gift is a seed that needs to be cultivated through prayer, dedication and constant exercise. Thus, the apostle warns us in 1 Corinthians 13:8: "Charity never faileth: but whether there be prophecies, they shall fail; whether there be tongues, they shall cease; whether there be knowledge, it shall vanish away."

This means that when the perfect comes, some gifts will cease to manifest. But until that day, they are indispensable; they are the language of the Spirit, the instruments that enable us to fulfill God's mission, and the living signs that He is still at work in the midst of His Church. Every manifestation of a gift is a reminder that the body of Christ is being prepared for the glorious coming of the Lord.

Biblical Principles on the Duration of Gifts
I have learned that the Bible teaches us several essential aspects about when and how gifts operate in our lives:

1. **Irrevocability While We Are in Christ.** Gifts do not fade as long as we remain in community with the Lord. As Romans 11:29 says, God's grace remains constant and His gifts irrevocable.

2. **Development and exercise.** Paul exhorts us, "Therefore I counsel you to fan the fire of the

gift of God which is in you" (2 Timothy 1:6). This has motivated me not to let the gift God has entrusted to me rest, but to exercise and cultivate it continually in my life.

3. **Temporality of certain gifts at the end of the age.** While gifts are essential to our mission today, some, such as prophecy or tongues, will cease when the perfect is fulfilled, according to 1 Corinthians 13:8. This is a reminder that every gift has its time and purpose.

4. **Essential to the Church's current mission.** As long as the Church is on earth, gifts are needed to edify the saints, as expressed in Ephesians 4:12.

Biblical Examples of the Duration of Gifts

Scripture has shown me experiential examples of how gifts are kept active in those who serve God faithfully:

- **Moses**, who, despite his human limitations, led Israel to the end of his life (Deuteronomy 34:7).

- **Samuel**, who with the prophetic gift, spoke in God's name throughout his life (1 Samuel 3:19-20).

- **Paul**, whose gift of teaching was never extinguished, and who preached fervently until the end of his ministry (2 Timothy 4:6-8).

Each of these examples inspires me to see my own gifts as a call to serve and to remain active in God's work, no matter the circumstances.

Historical and Cultural Context

In Greco-Roman times, gifts were considered simple skills or talents acquired through training. But biblical teaching breaks with that view by revealing to us that spiritual gifts are, in fact, supernatural manifestations of the Holy Spirit. Today, we continue to face similar challenges:

- **Confusion between talent and gift:** Many times it is thought that these gifts are just personal skills.

- **Lack of discernment:** It is vital to learn to distinguish between what authentically comes from the Spirit and what is mere imitation.

- **Disconnection from mission:** Some believers forget to use these gifts to build up the body of Christ and fulfill the mission of the gospel.

The Latter Rain: Unleashing the Gifts for the End Time!

Ellen G. White's words have profoundly shaped my understanding of the enduring presence of spiritual gifts within the Church. In The Great Controversy, she affirms that as long as the Church remains on earth, the gifts of the Spirit will continue to operate for the edification of God's people.

This declaration underscores a fundamental truth: the work of the Holy Spirit is not confined to a specific era or generation but remains active and essential for the Church's mission. The gifts of the Spirit are divinely appointed to strengthen, guide, and equip believers, ensuring that the body of Christ continues to grow in faith and effectiveness.

Recognizing this reality calls us to embrace and cultivate the spiritual gifts entrusted to us. As stewards of God's grace, we are responsible for discerning, developing, and utilizing these gifts for His glory and the advancement of His kingdom. The Church does not rely solely on human wisdom or effort but thrives through the supernatural empowerment of the Holy Spirit.

Therefore, we must remain receptive to His guidance, faithfully exercising the gifts He has bestowed, and committing ourselves to the ongoing work of edification and transformation within the body of Christ.

Furthermore, in *Steps to Christ*, she emphasized that as long as God has given talents and gifts to every believer, but it is the responsibility of each to cultivate them and use them for His glory.

These reminders encourage me not to take lightly the gift God has entrusted to me, but to work actively in its development and application, always remembering that my service is for the glory of God and the benefit of His Church.

I invite you to meditate on the following, both personally and as a community:

Questions for Personal Reflection:
1. Have you identified the spiritual gifts God has given you since your conversion?

2. How can you use your gifts for the edification of the Church and the spread of the gospel?

3. Are you allowing the Holy Spirit to guide your service, or are you leaning more on your own abilities?

4. What can you do to avoid falling into pride or unnecessary competition when manifesting your gifts?

Questions for Community Discernment:
1. Is our Church promoting the use of spiritual gifts equitably among its members?

2. How can we help new believers discover and apply their gifts?

3. Are we focused on supporting the transforming work of the Holy Spirit, rather than relying solely on organizational structures?

At the end of the day, this meditation reminds me that spiritual gifts are the very language of the Spirit, the tools through which God operates in the world, and that they remain as long as we are in Christ. As long as we cultivate our gifts with love, discipline, and total dependence on the Holy Spirit, we will be instruments of edification in the body of Christ, until the glorious return of our Lord. How can you today renew your commitment to the transforming power of your gifts and serve with passion in God's mission? May this reflection inspire you to walk in the fullness of the grace that God has bestowed upon you.

This study reminds us that spiritual gifts are **manifestations of the Holy Ghost**, bestowed by the Father and guided by the Son. Every believer has a fundamental role in the body of Christ. How can we make sure we are using our gifts for the glory of God and the growth of His Church?

The Latter Rain: Unleashing the Gifts for the End Time!

Chapter 4: Understanding Spiritual Gifts

Description of Spiritual Gifts

When I reflect on spiritual gifts, I realize that immersing myself in their description is like stepping into the heavenly throne room. It is in that sacred space that God distributes unique jewels to each of us, gifts of grace that respond to the diverse needs of the body of Christ. Each gift is not simply a human skill, but a manifestation of the Spirit meant to enable us to do the work of building with efficiency, unity, and power.

God's Word reveals that there are more than twenty spiritual gifts, embodied throughout passages such as Romans 12, 1 Corinthians 12, Ephesians 4, and 1 Peter 4. This is not a closed list, but a broad testimony of God's inexhaustible creativity to operate in the lives of his children.

Classification of Spiritual Gifts

In my research and meditation, I have learned that gifts are grouped into various categories, each serving a specific function within the Church:

To delve into the study of spiritual gifts is to discover how God, in His infinite wisdom, has provided each believer with unique tools to build the Church and fulfill the mission of the Kingdom.

It is as if as we enter the heavenly throne room, each of us receives a different jewel, designed to meet particular needs and to enhance the work God has entrusted to us. It then expands and deepens the classification of these gifts according to their roles in the Church:

1. Gifts of Service (Romans 12:6-8)

These gifts are characterized by the ability to serve in practical and compassionate ways within the community of faith. Its purpose is not to elevate the individual, but to strengthen the body of Christ:

- Prophecy: It is understood as the ability to authoritatively declare God's will, interpret it, and communicate it to the people. It is not simply a matter of predicting the future, but of speaking divine truth in times of need, announcing light and hope when darkness prevails. Prophecy, in this sense, is a spiritual guide that alerts and strengthens the community.

- Service: This gift is manifested in a genuine willingness to assist in the practical needs of others and of the Church. It is an attitude of dedication that translates into concrete actions: caring for the sick, assisting the needy, and collaborating in the daily tasks that make the functioning of God's home possible.

- Teaching: The gift of teaching goes beyond transmitting knowledge; It involves explaining and applying biblical truth clearly and effectively. It is an art that opens minds and transforms hearts, enabling believers to understand the Scriptures and apply them to their daily lives, so that faith is translated into practice.

- Exhortation: This gift is often reflected in the ability to encourage, encourage, and strengthen members of the community. The exhortation is manifested in words that edify, motivate and, above all, invite us to a life of fidelity and commitment to God.

- Generosity: Generosity is expressed in the ease of giving with joy and detachment, without expecting anything in return. It is not only a material giving, but also a commitment of time, resources and energy to sustain the church and serve those in need, evidencing God's unconditional love.

- Leadership: This gift involves the ability to lead diligently and responsibly. It is not about imposing, but about leading with humility, wisdom, and a vision centered on the well-being of the body of Christ. Leadership in the spiritual realm fosters community growth, coordination, and unity.

- Mercy: Mercy reflects a compassionate heart, willing to show sincere care for others. It is the act of putting oneself in the place of one's neighbor, of offering comfort in moments of pain and of acting with empathy in the face of difficulties, following the example of love and forgiveness that Jesus left us.

2. Supernatural Gifts (1 Corinthians 12:8-10)

These gifts evidence the supernatural power of the Holy Spirit, manifesting itself in ways that transcend natural human capacities:

- Word of wisdom: It is the ability to apply divine knowledge effectively and pertinently in complex situations. Those who possess this gift are able to see solutions and paths based on God's perspective, offering counsel that illuminates and directs difficult situations.

- Word of knowledge: This gift allows us to understand and discern profound spiritual mysteries. Through revelations that go beyond human knowledge, those who possess this ability can understand truths about God's character and spiritual reality, communicating them in edifying ways.

- Faith: The gift of faith consists in trusting God in an extraordinary way, even in circumstances that reject all human logic. This supernatural faith impels us to act in situations that require deep conviction and total surrender to the divine will.

- Healing: Healing is the restorative power of the Spirit that manifests itself to heal sickness and disease. Beyond medicine, this ability reflects divine intervention to bring physical restoration and often a testimony of God's love and power in the midst of suffering.

- Miracles: They are manifestations of God's supernatural power that break with the normality of the natural world. Miracles are signs that confirm God's presence, testifying to His authority and His ability to intervene in history.

- Prophecy (supernatural): Although prophecy is also among the gifts of service, in this context it acquires a dimension that goes further, being the ability to receive and proclaim direct revelations from God with an authority that transcends the ordinary.

- Discernment of spirits: This ability allows us to identify and distinguish between spiritual influences. Those who possess this gift can recognize the presence of evil or confirm the authenticity of what comes from the Holy Spirit, protecting the community from deception.

- Tongues: It is the gift of speaking in unknown languages in a natural way, without the need for prior learning, as a sign of the inspiration of the Spirit. This gift serves to edify believers and to manifest the power of God in a visible way.

- Interpretation of tongues: Complementary to the gift of tongues, this is the gift of translating and clarifying these messages in unknown languages, so that the whole community can be edified and understand the message that God wants to transmit.

3. Ministerial Gifts (Ephesians 4:11)
These gifts are specifically geared toward building up the Church and spreading the gospel, focusing on ministry roles and spiritual leadership:

- Apostles: Those called to be church founders and overseers. Its mission is to establish and support communities of faith, marking the beginning of church movements that transcend borders.

- Prophets (ministerial): They are special messengers who communicate God's designs in a direct and authoritative way, providing clarity and direction in critical moments for the Church.

- Evangelists: This gift is responsible for bringing the message of the gospel to those who have not yet been reached, igniting in them the desire to know Christ and be part of the body.

- Pastors: With the role of caring for and spiritually guiding the congregation, these leaders are dedicated to nurturing, protecting, and strengthening the faith community, ensuring its stability and spiritual growth.

- Teachers: They are charged with instructing believers in Christian doctrine, deepening their understanding of God's Word and preparing them for effective service within the body.

4. Gifts of Administration and Help (1 Peter 4:10)

These gifts facilitate the practical and logistical functioning of the Church, making it possible for all efforts to be efficiently coordinated:

- Administration: The ability to effectively organize and direct the resources and energies of the community. Those who have this gift ensure that every aspect of church life flows in an orderly manner, allowing the mission to be carried out effectively.

- Help: This gift manifests itself in a humble attitude and willingness to serve, facilitating continuous support to the community. It is the gift of being present in every need, offering assistance and care in a compassionate and selfless way.

Biblical Examples of Gifts in Action

As I review the scriptures, I find inspiring examples that illustrate how God bestowed and used these gifts for His glory:

- Moses and Leadership (Exodus 3:10-12): Although initially doubtful, Moses was called, equipped, and guided by God to lead Israel out of bondage, demonstrating leadership that transformed an entire nation.

- Bezalel and Oholiab (Exodus 31:1-6): These craftsmen were endowed with the gift of craftsmanship. With great skill, they contributed to the construction of the tabernacle, showing how God-inspired creativity creates sacred structures for worshiping Him.

- Peter and the gift of preaching (Acts 2:14-41): At Pentecost, Peter, filled with the power of the Spirit, proclaimed the gospel and led thousands to the way of salvation, showing the impact of a gift that transcends the merely verbal.

- Paul and the Gift of Teaching (Romans 1:1; 1 Timothy 2:7): The apostle Paul, through his deep understanding of the Word, doctrinally formed the Church, laying firm foundations for future generations of believers.

Reflection

The diversity of spiritual gifts is a testament to the richness of God's grace and His desire to see a vibrant and united Church, where each member has a unique and essential role. As you reflect on your own gifts or observe how they operate in your community, I encourage you to ponder the following questions:

Questions for Personal Reflection:

1. Have you identified the spiritual gifts God has given you and understood His purpose in your life?

2. How can you use your gifts to build up the Church and for the gospel to reach more people?

3. Do you trust the guidance of the Holy Ghost as you exercise your gift, or do you lean more on your own abilities?

4. What concrete steps can you take to avoid falling into pride and competition and thus serve humbly and effectively?

Questions for Community Discernment:
1. Is our Church promoting the equitable use of spiritual gifts among all its members?

2. How can we help new believers discover and exercise the gifts the Holy Spirit has entrusted to them?

3. Are we directing our efforts toward the transforming work of the Spirit, rather than relying solely on human organizational structures?

May this deep exploration of spiritual gifts inspire you to see in every manifestation of the Spirit an invitation to serve, to grow in unity, and to be a living force for the glory of God. Remember that your gifts are not merely talents but powerful tools of the Kingdom that, used in love and humility, build a vibrant body of Christ, ready to take the message of salvation to every corner of the world.

Each one received a specific gift, destined to fulfill a concrete task within God's eternal plan.

Historical and Cultural Context
In my journey of faith, I have come to discover that, in the Greco-Roman era, gifts were simply understood as natural abilities or talents acquired through rigorous training. However, as I delved into God's Word, I understood that biblical teaching

invites us to look further: spiritual gifts are supernatural manifestations of the Holy Spirit, heavenly gifts that transform our lives and enable us to participate in the eternal work of the Kingdom.

Today, many in the Church still confuse spiritual gifts with mere human abilities. Sometimes I hear it said that it is a matter of talent or skill, forgetting that these gifts are the fruit of divine grace. The lack of discernment in the face of what truly comes from the Spirit and what is simply an imitation has generated a disconnect in the use of these gifts. Some brothers and sisters do not use their gifts for the edification of the body of Christ, losing sight of the fact that each gift is given to serve others and glorify God.

Ellen G. White's words have illuminated my understanding of this reality. In *The Great Controversy*, she states that God has endowed His Church with diverse talents, and each one is to be employed for His glory. The work of God is not advanced by the efforts of a few, but by the cooperation of all.

Additionally, in *Steps to Christ*, she reminds me that, when the members of the Church work in harmony, each using the gifts God has given him, the body of Christ is strengthened and the gospel advances with power.

These inspiring words impel me to always seek unity in diversity and to recognize that the true power of the gospel is manifested in a body of faith where we all collaborate selflessly. God, in His infinite wisdom, does not arbitrarily dole out gifts, but each gift is a unique jewel meant to meet the diverse needs of the body of Christ.

As I contemplate the description of spiritual gifts, I realize that each of these gifts is a manifestation of God's grace for a specific purpose. Knowing them and understanding their true nature is not only an informative exercise, but a transformative act that impels us to discern which of these gifts the Spirit has deposited in us and how we can put them at the service of the Kingdom.

I would like to invite you to reflect on your own journey and that of our community of faith.

Questions for Personal Reflection:
1. Have you identified the spiritual gifts God has entrusted to you?

2. How can you use these gifts to build up the Church and spread the gospel around you?

3. Are you allowing the Holy Spirit to guide your service, or are you overly relying on your own abilities?

4. What concrete steps could you take to avoid falling into pride or competition in the manifestation of your gifts?

Questions for Community Discernment:

1. Is our Church promoting the use of spiritual gifts in a fair and equitable manner among its members?

2. How can we help new believers discover, exercise, and apply the gifts the Spirit has bestowed upon them?

3. Are we devoting our efforts to the true work of the Holy Spirit, or are we still clinging to organizational structures that limit our flexibility to act?

Each gift is an invitation to serve, to be an active part of a vibrant, united body that manifests God's power in the world. By embracing the diversity of these gifts and putting them at the service of the Kingdom, we become living witnesses of divine love and grace that transforms the human heart. May this meditation inspire you to shine forth the gift that the Spirit has entrusted to you, so that together we can build a Church that moves forward with passion and unity, honoring God in every act of service.

Chapter 5: The Dynamics of Spiritual Gifts

Throughout my walk in faith, I have come to understand that spiritual gifts are much more than mere skills or ornaments to our existence. They are dynamic, deeply practical, relational gifts, flowing from the same Spirit to build up the body of Christ. Imagining myself entering the heavenly throne room, where the Spirit distributes unique jewels to each believer, fills me with awe and gratitude. Each gift is designed to fulfill a divine purpose: to enable the Church to act in unity, in love, and in mission.

The Bible teaches me that these gifts are not hidden in passivity; They operate in continuous movement and growth. As Romans 12:6 says, "Having then gifts differing according to the grace that is given to us, whether prophecy, let us prophesy according to the proportion of faith." This reminds me that God expects us to practice and exercise our gifts, not to keep them idle. It is in this daily action that every gift flourishes and becomes an instrument of life for the body of Christ.

Over time I have come to understand that no gift acts alone. As Romans 12:4 says, " For as we have many members in one body, and all members have not the same office," each gift is interrelated with the others to form a living and harmonious organism. I have seen up close that when my gifts are exercised in communion with those of others, they multiply and have greater impact. Without love, as 1 Corinthians 13:1 teaches us, every manifestation of a gift becomes hollow, like metal that resonates without finding meaning.

I also recognize that gifts, like a seed, can develop and grow if properly nurtured. Paul's exhortation in 2 Timothy 1:6, "Wherefore I put thee in remembrance that thou stir up the gift of God, which is in thee by the putting on of my hands," prompts me not to let my gift atrophy, but to exercise and strengthen it through active service and constant devotion.

I can vividly remember the thrilling example of the disciples at Pentecost, when they were all filled with the Spirit and began to manifest gifts in miraculous ways (Acts 2:1-4). Those powerful images of conversion and transformation inspire me to believe that, as a believer, I, too, have been equipped to fulfill a specific task in God's work. Conversion marks the beginning of a call in which our gifts come to put God's will into action.

Looking at the historical context, I realize that in Greco-Roman times gifts were understood as natural abilities or skills acquired through rigorous training. However, biblical teaching challenges us to look beyond, revealing to us that spiritual gifts are supernatural manifestations of the Holy Spirit.

The Latter Rain: Unleashing the Gifts for the End Time!

Today, in the midst of a culture that sometimes confuses talent with gift, it is vital to discern the difference and not lose sight of the mission that God has entrusted to us: to build up the Church.

In this regard, Ellen G. White's inspiring words have been a light in my life. In *The Great Controversy* she said that when the members of the Church are fully consecrated to the work of God, the Holy Spirit will be poured out in abundant measure, and the work of God will go forward with power.

Additionally, in *Steps to Christ*, it is noted also that when the members of the Church work in harmony, each using the gifts God has given him, the body of Christ is strengthened and the gospel advances with power. These truths constantly encourage me to seek that unity in the diversity of gifts, reminding me that the true power of the gospel lies in the collaboration of all of us to fulfill God's mission.

I would like to share with you some of the gifts that are grouped into different categories and that I have discovered along the way:

Gifts of Service: These include prophecy, which is the ability to authoritatively declare God's will, as well as teaching, which allows us to explain and apply biblical truth in transformative ways. It is also manifested in exhortation, a gift that encourages and strengthens the believer; in service, which teaches to help with practical needs; in generosity, which inspires us to give with joy; in leadership, which calls us to guide diligently; and in mercy, which is expressed in sincere care for others.

Supernatural Gifts: These are gifts that go beyond human understanding, such as the word of wisdom and knowledge, that equip us with understanding deep spiritual truths. The gift of faith impels us to trust God against all odds, while healing and miracles are tangible manifestations of God's power to restore and transform. In addition, we are given the gift of tongues and their interpretation, which serve to edify the community through inspired and clear messages, and the discernment of spirits, which helps us distinguish between truly divine influences and those that mimic the sacred.

Ministerial Gifts: These gifts, such as apostle, prophet, evangelist, pastor, and teacher, are meant to build up the Church, guide believers, and take the gospel to those who do not yet know it, thus forming a robust spiritual leadership that sustains the whole body.

Gifts of Administration and Help: Finally, administration and the gift of help are manifested in the ability to organize, direct, and assist in a humble and selfless way, making every effort be done with efficiency and love.

As I meditate on the diversity of these gifts, I am reminded of biblical examples that illuminate their power: Moses was an extraordinary leader, Bezalel and Oholiab had the artistic skills to build the tabernacle, Peter renewed the life of the Church at Pentecost with his preaching, and Paul, with his gift of teaching, formed generations of believers.

I invite you to join me in a sincere reflection on your own journey:
- Have you identified the spiritual gifts God has entrusted to you?

- How can you use these gifts to build up the Church and radically spread the gospel?

- Do you allow the Holy Spirit to guide you, or do you lean more on your own abilities, forgetting the true source of power?

- What practical steps can you take to prevent pride or competition from obscuring the beauty of your gift?

And at the community level, let us ask ourselves together:
- Is our Church promoting the equitable use of gifts among all its members?

- How can we help new believers discover and apply the wonders the Spirit has given them?

- Are we putting our trust in the transforming work of the Holy Spirit, letting go of organizational structures that limit our potential?

Contemplating the dynamics of spiritual gifts reminds me every day that, far from being static or decorative, these gifts are alive and in constant motion, impelling the Church to be an effective instrument of the kingdom of God. May this personal meditation inspire you to embrace the diversity of gifts, to discover the unique jewel that the Spirit has placed in your life, and to share it with passion, wisdom, and love so that the gospel may advance with power in every corner of the world.

This study reminds us that spiritual gifts are **manifestations of the Holy Ghost**, bestowed by the Father and guided by the Son. Every believer has a fundamental role in the body of Christ. How can we make sure we are using our gifts for the glory of God and the growth of His Church?

Gifts and Spiritual Leadership

In my journey in faith, I have come to understand that leadership in the Church is not simply a matter of titles or merely human abilities, but is grounded in the evidence of the spiritual gifts conferred by the Holy Ghost. In my personal experience, I have seen how a pastor who possesses the gift of pastoring, teaching, and leadership becomes a true servant who leads the community with love and wisdom, while an elder who demonstrates wisdom and exhortation becomes the beacon that illuminates and guides others in times of uncertainty. This conviction has led me to firmly believe that every ecclesiastical office must be backed by the corresponding gift in order to faithfully fulfill the mission God assigns.

As I reflect on Scripture, I find in Ephesians 4:11 that " And he gave some, apostles; and some, prophets; and some, evangelists; and some, pastors and teachers," which teaches me that God, in His sovereignty, assigns leaders based on specific spiritual gifts. This means that true leadership is not based on human criteria or social status, but on the manifestation of the Spirit in one's life. I remember clearly how in Acts 6:3 – "Wherefore, brethren, look ye out among you seven men of honest report, full of the Holy Ghost and wisdom, whom we may appoint over this business," we are exhorted to seek leaders filled with the Spirit and wisdom, which makes me think about the importance of our leaders reflecting deep fellowship with God.

I have also learned that leadership must be exercised with humility and a spirit of service, just as Jesus taught us in Matthew 20:27: " And whosoever will be chief among you, let him be your servant." Personally, I have experienced the difference when I lead from a heart full of service rather than seeking personal exaltation. Every time I cultivate my gift and allow the Holy Spirit to activate it, I find a joy that transcends any human recognition, because I know that I am doing it to build up the body of Christ.

Another truth that has marked me is the importance of continually reviving the gift that God has entrusted to me; in 2 Timothy 1:6 we are exhorted to "fan the fire of the gift of God that is in you." This means that as leaders, we must not let the passion to serve cool down, but we must always seek spiritual renewal to exercise our calling effectively. In my own ministry, I have learned to depend more on the power of the Spirit than on my own abilities, recognizing that without Him, our efforts fall short.

The Bible gives us numerous examples of leaders who served with clearly evidenced gifts:

1. Moses was called and equipped by God to lead Israel (Exodus 3:10-12), showing me that effective leadership comes from a deep dependence on God.

2. Solomon, with the gift of wisdom, ruled with divine discernment (1 Kings 3:9-12), teaching me that wisdom is vital to making just and compassionate decisions. Peter, with his gift of preaching, lit the flame of the gospel at Pentecost (Acts 2:14-41), demonstrating that the power of God's word can transform multitudes.

3. Paul, through the gift of teaching, doctrinally formed generations of believers (Romans 1:1; 1 Timothy 2:7), leaving me a legacy of ministry instruction that still inspires me to continue to deepen my understanding of the Word.

As for the historical and cultural context, I remember that in the Greco-Roman world, leadership was defined by social status and the natural ability acquired through training, a totally different perspective from the truth revealed in the Bible. Today, many still fall into the trap of choosing leaders by social influence, forgetting that the divine call is manifested in the presence of the Spirit and in the evidence of spiritual gifts. This blurring generates what I have seen in my ministry: a disconnect between leadership and the genuine service that God desires for His people.

Ellen G. White's inspiring words have helped me deepen this understanding. I remember that in *The Great Controversy* she wrote that when the leaders of the Church work in harmony, each using the gifts God has given him, the body of Christ is strengthened and the gospel advances with power.

And in *Step to Christ*, we are reminded again that without the Holy Spirit, the gifts cannot operate effectively. It is divine power that transforms human talents into tools for the glory of God. words prompt me to evaluate my own leadership and to motivate myself to help others discover and cultivate the gifts the Spirit has given them.

I invite you to reflect on your personal life:
1. Have you identified the spiritual gifts God has entrusted to you for leadership?

2. How can you use these gifts to build up the Church and promote the spread of the gospel?

3. Are you allowing the Holy Spirit to guide your leadership, or are you relying more on your own abilities?

4. What concrete steps can you take to avoid pride or competition in exercising your spiritual leadership?

And at the community level, let's think together:

1. Is our Church promoting leadership based on genuine spiritual gifts and not merely human criteria?

2. How can we help new leaders discover their gifts and apply them for the benefit of the community?

3. Are we focusing on the transforming work of the Holy Spirit rather than clinging to rigid organizational structures?

Each of these challenges and reflections reminds me that spiritual leadership is nurtured by humility, total dependence on God, and the active manifestation of the gifts that the Holy Spirit pours out. We are called not only to lead, but to serve, to build one another up, and to advance the mission God has entrusted to us. May this call inspire you to lead with passion, wisdom, and a caring heart, in perfect harmony with the Spirit and for the glory of God.

This study reminds us that leadership in the Church must be **supported by spiritual gifts** and guided by the Holy Ghost. Every believer has a fundamental role in the body of Christ. How can we make sure we are using our gifts for the glory of God and the growth of His Church?

Practical Gifts and Ministries

In my walk with Christ, I have discovered that spiritual gifts are not limited to the classrooms of doctrine or theological rituals; they go much further. I have felt these divine gifts manifest in very practical ways in the life of the Church, from the powerful message that saves souls to the tender act of welcoming a visitor on the threshold of a temple. Every practical ministry—whether hospitality, intercession, financial aid, spiritual accompaniment, or evangelism—is an opportunity to let the Holy Spirit guide our actions and make us living testimonies of His love.

I remember when, in one of those intense moments of prayer, I understood that hospitality was not only a courtesy, but a ministry that opens the heart of the Church to one's neighbor, offering a warm and affectionate atmosphere that makes the divine presence palpable. Likewise, I have witnessed the gift of intercession multiply in prayer teams, where fervor and unity in spiritual battle become a wall of hope for those going through difficult times.

The Bible calls us to use each gift for the common good. In 1 Peter 4:10 we are reminded: "As every man hath received the gift, even so minister the same one to another, as good stewards of the manifold grace of God."

This verse has been a constant in my life and has taught me that our gifts, whether they are to exhort, teach, or even to take the gospel through public campaigns or through social media, must be exercised diligently.

As Romans 12:6 tells us: " Having then gifts differing according to the grace that is given to us, whether prophecy, let us prophesy according to the proportion of faith."

Here the emphasis is on the need not to keep our gifts in silence, but to put them into action in favor of a united Church committed to its mission.

I have come to see that nothing we do is isolated. Just as in a body each member has his function, in the Church each gift is indispensable. No one can minister in isolation, because we all work in interdependence, as Romans 12:4 teaches us: "For as we have many members in one body, and all members have not the same office."

Without love, without that motivation whose source is the heart transformed by Christ, even the most impressive gift remains empty. Remember what Paul says in 1 Corinthians 13:1, that vocalization without love is like metal that simply resounds without producing fruit.

I have also learned that gifts can flourish or, neglected, atrophy. That's why I try daily to "fan the fire of the gift of God that is in me" (2 Timothy 1:6), because practice makes our gifts develop and be effective, transforming our lives and the community around us.

The Bible gives us beautiful practical examples of how these gifts materialized at key moments in the history of the Church. I am reminded of the work of Bezalel and Oholiab, who used their gift of craftsmanship to build the tabernacle, a sacred meeting place, in Exodus 31:1-6. I also think of the early deacons of the early Church, who organized and served those in need, demonstrating that service is a tangible manifestation of God's love. And I can't forget Peter's powerful preaching at Pentecost (Acts 2:14-41) and Paul's teaching ministry (Acts 19:8-10), examples of how each gift plays a specific role in God's work.

As I reflect on this context, I realize that in the Greco-Roman world, gifts were conceived simply as natural abilities or acquired skills. But biblical revelation shows us that these gifts are, in fact, supernatural manifestations of the Holy Spirit. Today, the Church faces similar challenges: there is a confusion between human talent and spiritual gift, and sometimes we even ignore the true mission of building up the body of Christ.

White said that when the members of the Church are fully consecrated to the work of God, the Holy Ghost will be poured out in an abundant measure, and the work of God will go forward with power.

And she also reminds us that when the members of the Church work in harmony, each using the gifts God has given him, the body of Christ is strengthened and the gospel advances with power.

These words inspire me to seek, both in my personal life and in my community, a full dependence on the transforming power of the Spirit.

I invite you to join me in a sincere reflection on our journey:

Questions for Personal Reflection:
1. Have you identified the spiritual gifts God has entrusted to you?

2. How can you use these gifts to build up the Church and spread the gospel around you?

3. Are you letting the Holy Spirit guide every action of your service, or are you leaning on your own abilities?

4. What steps can you take to prevent pride or competition from tarnishing the true calling of your gift?

Questions for Community Discernment:
1. Is our Church promoting the use of spiritual gifts equitably among all members?

2. How might we help new believers discover and apply these wonderful gifts of the Spirit?

3. Are we more focused on rigid organizational structures or on allowing the work of the Holy Spirit to flow freely to build up the body of Christ?

Each of us has received from the Spirit a unique jewel destined to transform our environment. As we integrate our gifts into the practice of the Church, we become a living body, active, and deeply dependent on the power of the Spirit. May this reflection motivate you to shine your gift for the glory of God, serving with passion, wisdom, and love in your community of faith.

This study reminds us that spiritual gifts are **manifestations of the Holy Ghost**, bestowed by the Father and guided by the Son. Every believer has a fundamental role in the body of Christ. How can we make sure we are using our gifts for the glory of God and the growth of His Church?

Gifts and Unity of the Body

In the course of my journey of faith, I have come to understand that one of the most beautiful fruits of the fullness of spiritual gifts is unity. I remember with amazement how, as we studied the Word, Paul revealed to us that "2 For as the body is one, and hath many members, and all the members of that one body, being many, are one body: so also is Christ" (1 Corinthians 12:12).

That image had a profound impact on me, for it made me see that when each member exercises the gift that God has entrusted to him, envy, comparison, and apathy disappear, and in their place a divine interdependence arises: he who teaches needs the one who serves, the one who exhorts needs the one who intercesses, and the one who leads depends on the one who administers. It is in that harmonious diversity that the body of Christ grows healthy and strong.

I have learned that the Bible teaches us essential principles about how gifts strengthen unity in the Church. For example, I understand that each member is indispensable, as it says in 1 Corinthians 12:18: "But now hath God set the members every one of them in the body, as it hath pleased him."

There is no superfluous believer, because each one has his or her unique role within the great divine design. Likewise, I know that the gifts must operate in perfect harmony.

The Latter Rain: Unleashing the Gifts for the End Time!

In 1 Corinthians 12:25 we are exhorted to act in such a way "That there should be no schism in the body; but that the members should have the same care one for another." This unity is based on the perfect bond of love, as Colossians 3:14 reminds us: " And above all these things put on charity, which is the bond of perfectness."

It is in that love that the gifts find their true purpose: to build up and not to divide, as emphasized in Ephesians 4:12, which tells us that the gifts are given " For the perfecting of the saints, for the work of the ministry, for the edifying of the body of Christ."

In the course of my studies, I have found in the history of the Church and in the biblical accounts examples that perfectly illustrate how this unity is manifested. I remember the days of Pentecost, when the disciples were filled with the Holy Spirit and began to manifest gifts in complete unity (Acts 2:1-4).

I am also thinking of the work of deacons in the early Church, who, by stewarding resources and caring for those in need (Acts 6:1-7), strengthened the community. And I can't forget how Paul, along with his co-workers, showed that leadership and service complement each other (Romans 16:1-16).

By transferring this reality to the historical and cultural context, I realize that in the Greco-Roman world society was hierarchically structured, with marked divisions between classes and roles. The early Church, however, broke with that scheme, promoting equality among its members, establishing a community where faith and shared service were the true hallmarks. Today, the Church faces similar challenges: Our modern world often emphasizes individualism and religious consumerism, and doctrinal fragmentation sometimes breeds divisions rather than unity.

In moments of deep reflection, I find comfort in the inspiring words of Ellen G. White. In *The Great Controversy* I read that when the members of the Church work in harmony, each using the gifts God has given him, the body of Christ is strengthened and the gospel advances with power. She also said that without the Holy Spirit, the gifts cannot operate effectively. It is divine power that transforms human talents into tools for the glory of God.

These words encourage me to always seek that unity in diversity, to allow my gifts and those of my brothers and sisters to be integrated into one body guided by the Spirit. It is not a matter of highlighting the individual, but of recognizing that every skill, whether it is the ability to teach, serve, lead, or intercede, has its reason for being and contributes to the building up of the body of Christ.

I invite you to reflect on these questions in your personal life and in your faith community:

Questions for Personal Reflection:
1. Have you identified the spiritual gifts God has given you?

2. How can you use your gifts to strengthen unity in your faith community?

3. Are you allowing the Holy Spirit to guide your service, or are you overly relying on your own abilities?

4. What steps can you take to avoid pride or competition in the exercise of your gifts?

Questions for Community Discernment:
1. Is our Church promoting the use of spiritual gifts equitably among its members?

2. How can we help new believers discover and apply their gifts?

3. Are we putting our trust in the transforming work of the Holy Spirit, rather than rigid organizational structures?

Each gift is a living manifestation of the Spirit, a gift that unites us all in a vibrant, mission-driven body. By recognizing and applying what the Spirit has placed in us, we contribute not only to our personal edification but also to the strength and growth of the body of Christ. How can you shine today the gift that the Spirit has entrusted to you for the glory of God and the growth of His Church? May this reflection inspire you to embrace unity in diversity, and to serve with humility, wisdom, and above all, with unwavering love.

This study reminds us that spiritual gifts are **manifestations of the Holy Ghost**, bestowed by the Father and guided by the Son. Every believer has a fundamental role in the body of Christ. How can we make sure we are using our gifts for the glory of God and the growth of His Church?

Global Gifts and Mission

For many years I have meditated deeply on the power of spiritual gifts and their essential role in the overall mission of the Church. I remember that in a moment of intense prayer, I was overcome with the certainty that good will is no longer enough; What is needed is the power of heaven working through consecrated vessels. That nascent revelation led me to understand that a Church that ignores its gifts is incomplete, while a Church that activates them becomes unstoppable, extending the kingdom of God beyond its borders.

I think of what the Word tells us in Mark 16:17-18: " And these signs shall follow them that believe; In my name shall they cast out devils; they shall speak with new tongues; They shall take up serpents; and if they drink any deadly thing, it shall not hurt them; they shall lay hands on the sick, and they shall recover."

These words, which resounded in my heart, showed me the magnitude of what it means to live under the power of the Spirit. It is not just about fine words, but about miracles, healings, and mass conversions, powerful manifestations of faith and discernment that lead us to believe that God's global mission is underway. The promise is clear: every gift manifested is an instrument of divine grace, a supernatural thrust that transforms lives and communities.

I've learned that everything starts in secret. It is in the silence of personal prayer, in the intimacy of our encounter with God, that every believer chooses to use his gift for the glory of the Most High. That decision, made deep within the soul, lays the foundation for the Holy Spirit to flow freely through us. And you, dear brother or sister, are also part of that great body. The Spirit desires to work through you, equipping you to be a living witness of companionship for Christ's mission on earth.

The Dynamics of Gifts and Global Mission

The Bible teaches us fundamental principles for understanding how spiritual gifts drive global mission:

1. Gifts are given to testify to God's power. In Acts 1:8, we are promised:

"You will receive power, when the Holy Spirit has come upon you, and you will be witnesses to me..." This reminds me that it is not just a call to live a life of faith, but to be bearers of God's power that transforms the world, bringing the message of salvation to every corner of the planet.

2. **Gifts strengthen evangelization.** Ephesians 4:12 explains that gifts are intended "to equip the saints for the work of the ministry, for the building up of the body of Christ." In my experience, this means that every grace granted is not a gift for personal gain, but a tool to share the gospel effectively and practically, through words and actions that inspire change.

3. **The latter rain will bring a revival of gifts.** The prophecy of Acts 2:17 and the vision of the outpouring of the Spirit resonate powerfully in my walk. Imagining that "latter rain" — the last great outpouring of the Spirit that will accompany miracles, healings, and mass conversions — fills me with hope. It is in that time of revival that the power of the gifts will multiply and the full manifestation of the Kingdom will become evident.

4. **Every believer has a role in global mission.** Remembering 1 Peter 4:10 makes me feel that there are no believers without gifts. Each person is intentionally empowered to serve and contribute, forming a mosaic of mercy, wisdom, leadership, and most of all, love. That interconnectedness is the force that makes the

Church unstoppable in the face of the challenges of our world.

Biblical Examples Illustrating This Mission
As I study the experiences of the early disciples, I am moved by the image of those who, being filled with the Spirit at Pentecost, began to manifest gifts in a united and powerful way (Acts 2:1-4). I am also reminded of Philip's ministry in Samaria, who, moved by the gift of evangelism, carried the message of God's love accompanied by miraculous signs, changing the lives of countless people (Acts 8:5-8).

I cannot forget how Paul, with the gift of teaching, built the Church in Ephesus during two intense years (Acts 19:8-10), and how Peter, through the gift of healing, performed miracles such as healing a lame man at the door of the temple (Acts 3:6-8). Each of these examples emphasizes to me that gifts are put into action to fulfill God's plan of redemption. they are not mere words, but palpable proofs of the power of the Holy Spirit at work in our midst.

Historical and Cultural Context
It is fascinating to note that in the Greco-Roman world the spread of a new faith depended heavily on charismatic messengers and leaders. However, biblical teaching breaks with that paradigm, affirming that God's mission depends on the power of the Holy Spirit and the manifestation of spiritual gifts.

Today, the Church faces challenges that are very similar to those of yesteryear:

- **Secularization:** Contemporary culture often alienates many people from the faith, making it difficult to convey the gospel message.

- **Spiritual indifference:** There are those who live without passion or urgency for mission, ignoring God's deep call to transform the world.

- **Need for unity:** Doctrinal fragmentation and individualism threaten to weaken the collective witness of the body of Christ.

As I question the direction of global mission, I return to the words of Mrs. White, I remember with gratitude her statement in that when the members of the Church are fully consecrated to the work of God, the Holy Ghost will be poured out in abundant measure, and the work of God will go forward with power. Also, I am reminded the latter rain will come upon those who, through faith and prayer, have prepared their hearts to receive it.

Not only do these teachings strengthen my conviction that God has a purpose for every gift, but they encourage me to prepare fervently for that great revival that is sure to transform lives and communities.

The Latter Rain: Unleashing the Gifts for the End Time!

I invite you, like me, to pause and reflect on the role that spiritual gifts play in God's mission. Consider these questions in your personal life and in the faith community:

Questions for Personal Reflection:
1. Have you identified the spiritual gifts God has given you for the Kingdom mission?

2. How can you use your gifts for evangelism and Kingdom growth?

3. Are you allowing the Holy Spirit to guide your ministry, or are you overly relying on your own abilities?

4. What concrete steps can you take to prepare for that latter rain that will revive your gift and the gift of others?

Questions for Community Discernment:
1. Is our Church focused on global mission, or is it distracted by secondary issues?

2. How can we foster deeper engagement and leadership imbued with the power of the Spirit for evangelism and service?

3. Are we actively praying and preparing to receive the latter rain and revival that God promised?

4. In what ways can we help believers discover and use their spiritual gifts to impact the communities around us?

Each gift is a unique manifestation of divine grace, a tool of transformation that equips us to bring the light of Christ to every corner of this world. By embracing and putting into action the gifts God has given us, we become relentless agents of change, committed to global mission.

May this meditation inspire you to be an active part of this mission, to allow the Spirit to flow through you, and to collaborate with a deep sense of community in building up the body of Christ. You too are a bearer of heavenly power, ready to make a difference in this world. How can you shine today the gift that the Spirit has entrusted to you for the glory of God and for the growth of His Church?

May love, faith, and unity always be the mark of your Christian Walk.

This study reminds us that spiritual gifts are **manifestations of the Holy Ghost**, bestowed by the Father and guided by the Son. Every believer has a critical role in global mission.

How can we make sure we are using our gifts for the glory of God and the growth of His Church?

Chapter 6: The Discovery of Spiritual Gifts

I have walked for years in search of the voice of the Spirit, and in that profound pilgrimage I discovered a glorious truth: God has placed a special gift in every believer. This seemingly simple notion is so transformative that it completely changed my view of ministry and the way I relate to the Church. It is not just about knowing that there is a gift, but about discovering what is the unique gift that the Spirit has deposited in us and putting it into action for the blessing of others.

"But the manifestation of the Spirit is given to every man to profit withal" (1 Corinthians 12:7).

These words filled me with hope and purpose. I understood that there is not a single believer without a gift. Each one of us has been trained to serve, to minister, to transform realities; for this, the gift is not a hidden mystery, but a manifestation of the same Spirit who impels us towards God's mission.

1. Biblical Principles on the Discovery of Gifts

The Bible clearly teaches us that spiritual gifts are not hidden in the shadows of the stranger, but are in the sight of those who are willing to receive and cultivate them. In that sense, I have learned that:

- **Every believer has at least one gift.** There is no person in God's family without God's ability to share in His grace, for "to each one is given the manifestation of the Spirit for profit" (1 Corinthians 12:7).

- Gifts must be discovered and used. Paul exhorts us:

"Wherefore I put thee in remembrance that thou stir up the gift of God, which is in thee by the putting on of my hands" (2 Timothy 1:6). This teaches me that if a gift is not exercised, it risks becoming inactive, and it is our responsibility as believers to keep that spark alive through prayer, study, and action.

- **The discovery of the gifts requires prayer and discernment.** In moments of stillness, when I have asked God for direction, I have remembered the teaching of James:

" If any of you lack wisdom, let him ask of God, that giveth to all men liberally, and upbraideth not; and it shall be given him" (James 1:5). Thus, the way to discover our gifts is made of intimate communion with the Father, asking for wisdom and allowing the Spirit to guide us.

- **The gifts must be confirmed in the community of faith.** Through interaction with mature leaders and believers, I have been able to see how God gives tangible signs of His work in our lives.

The warning of 1 Timothy 4:14 reminds me: "Neglect not the gift that is in thee, which was given thee by prophecy, with the laying on of the hands of the presbytery." The Church, as a body, has a crucial role to play in recognizing and activating what God has entrusted to us.

2. Steps to Discovering Spiritual Gifts

Discovering the gift God has placed in me has been a spiritual and practical process. Each step has become a step of faith that has led me to greater self-awareness and commitment to divine work:

- **Prayer and Spiritual Search.** In countless moments of solitude and prayer, I have asked the Lord to reveal to me the gift that He, in His infinite grace, has placed in me. These hours of personal fellowship have been instrumental in learning to listen to the Holy Spirit's leading.

- **Personal Evaluation.** I have paused to reflect on the areas in which I feel an unusual passion and natural efficacy. I ask myself: In what activities do I feel God's support? Where do I find peace and joy in serving? These questions have helped me identify divine clues about my gift.

- **Confirmation in the Community.** I have sought counsel from spiritual leaders and believers whom I respect and admire. Through their insight and recognition, I have been able to confirm those areas where my testimony and service seem to stand out, evidencing the Spirit's work in me.

- **Proof and Exercise of the Gift.** Finally, I have dared to actively participate in various ministries. I've experimented with different ways of serving, observing where God uses me with the greatest impact. Even in the stumbles, I have learned valuable lessons that have polished and strengthened my gift, understanding that there is no bad learning when acting in obedience.

Biblical Examples of Gift Discovery

The telling of biblical history is an inexhaustible source of inspiration. I think of characters like:

- **Moses,** who, despite his doubts, was called and equipped to lead Israel (Exodus 3:10-12).

- **Samuel,** who in his childhood learned to listen to God's voice, marking the beginning of his prophetic discernment (1 Samuel 3:1-10).

- **Paul,** one of the transformers of his life is evident after his conversion (Acts 9:15-20), and whose passion for teaching became a pillar for the edification of the Church.

- **Timothy,** who received his gift through the laying on of hands, showing that the community context is fundamental to validate and activate that divine gift (1 Timothy 4:14).

Each of these examples teaches me that the discovery of spiritual gifts is a process that not only reveals our identity in Christ, but also calls us to act with determination, so that God's work is manifested in our lives and around us.

4. Historical and Cultural Context

During the Greco-Roman era, gifts were understood simply as natural abilities or talents acquired by training. However, biblical revelation breaks with this limited perspective: spiritual gifts are supernatural manifestations of the Holy Spirit. Today, human talent is often still confused with the authentic divine gift. A lack of discernment in identifying the genuine work of the Spirit and a possible disconnect with the original mission of the Church are challenges that we continually face. These realities motivate me to pray and seek greater clarity to discern what is truly God's.

Mrs. White stated that when the members of the Church are fully consecrated to God's work, the

Holy Spirit will be poured out in abundant measure, propelling His mission forward with great power. When believers serve in unity, each utilizing the gifts entrusted to them by God, the body of Christ is strengthened, and the gospel advances with divine authority.

These teachings have encouraged me not only to seek the discovery of my gifts, but to exercise them in community, knowing that true strength is found in unity and selfless service that reflects the unconditional love of Christ.

At the conclusion of this journey of discovery, I invite you, dear friend, to stop and meditate on your spiritual journey. Some questions that have helped me to audit my own life are:

Questions for Personal Reflection:
1. Have you identified the spiritual gifts God has given you and feel His presence palpably in your life?

2. How can you use these gifts to build up the Church and spread the gospel, impacting those around you?

3. Are you letting the Holy Spirit guide your service, or are you sometimes overly reliant on your own skills and knowledge?

4. What concrete actions can you take to prevent pride or competition from clouding the beauty of your gift?

Questions for Community Discernment:
1. Is our Church promoting the effective and equitable use of spiritual gifts among all its members?

2. How can we help new believers discover, cultivate, and apply the gifts entrusted to them by the Holy Spirit?

3. Are we concentrating our efforts on allowing the Spirit's work to manifest freely, rather than getting stuck in organizational structures that limit our potential?

Each gift is a unique jewel of the Spirit, a divine gift that summons us to live in active and transformative ways. By discovering and exercising our gift, we not only fulfill God's call to us, but we also contribute to the edification and unity of the body of Christ. The task is challenging and requires humility, perseverance, and above all, unwavering trust in the power of the Holy Spirit.

May this meditation inspire you to embark on the exciting journey of discovering your spiritual gifts, and in doing so, may you find a new dimension of service and love in the mission God has entrusted to His Church. May the Spirit guide and strengthen you through every step of this wonderful process!

This study reminds us that **discovering spiritual gifts is a process of prayer, discernment, and action**. Every believer has a fundamental role in the body of Christ.

How can we make sure we are using our gifts for the glory of God and the growth of His Church?

In my walk with Christ, I have learned that using spiritual gifts in ways that glorify God and strengthen His Church is an ongoing process of intimacy, discernment, and maturity. The question we ask ourselves – how can we ensure that we are using our gifts for the glory of God and the growth of His Church? – has led me to reflect deeply on my own life and ministry.

I would like to share with you some considerations that have personally helped me to live according to the divine purpose of each gift.

Be born again

It all starts from the very foundation of the relationship with Christ. Spiritual gifts do not flow in a vacuum; They are for those who have experienced the new birth.

Remembering Paul's words in Romans 8:9: "But ye are not in the flesh, but in the Spirit, if so be that the Spirit of God dwell in you. Now if any man have not the Spirit of Christ, he is none of his."

If you have not yet given your life to Christ, everything else becomes unattainable. Conversion is the starting point that opens the channel through which the Spirit descends upon us, granting us not only salvation, but also the ability to serve with supernatural power. From my experience, when I discovered that my life was completely transformed by Christ, I began to see certain impulses and passions that previously seemed inexplicable, and I understood that these were the indications of a gift destined to be used for His glory.

Think You Have a Gift

Often, the inner struggle arises when we do not recognize and value the gift God has given us. The Bible assures us in 1 Corinthians 12:7: "But the manifestation of the Spirit is given to every man to profit withal."

God excludes no one. Remember that His promises are for all who believe. By believing that you have a gift, you open your heart to the possibility of its manifestation. A few years ago, I struggled to accept that God could have deposited a spiritual gift in me, but once I embraced that truth, I noticed an inner release and an openness to receive confirmation both personally and from others in the community.

Pray for discernment

Prayer is the essential bridge that connects us to the source of all our gifts. I have experienced moments of intense prayer in which I cry out, "Show me, Lord, how you have equipped me to serve." That sincere request is fundamental.

James 1:5 exhorts us: " If any of you lack wisdom, let him ask of God, that giveth to all men liberally, and upbraideth not; and it shall be given him."

It is in the stillness of prayer that the Spirit subtly reveals what areas He is working in you, and that, in turn, helps you discern your gift and guide you to use it correctly.

Study the Gifts in Depth

It is not enough to accept that you have a gift, but it is necessary to study and understand it in the light of Scripture. Take time to read and reread key passages such as Romans 12, 1 Corinthians 12, Ephesians 4, and 1 Peter 4. During this process of study, I have discovered how other believers have used their gifts throughout history and how those same principles apply today. Going deeper will give you a broader perspective on what it truly means to be an instrument of God, and it will help you align your ministry with God's plan.

Observe your natural inclination

God, in his wisdom, often aligns our gifts with our deepest inclinations, those godly desires that move us internally. Reflect honestly on activities in which you feel a special attraction or in which you experience surprising effectiveness. In my case, I have always felt a passion for service and spiritual accompaniment, which my community has confirmed as a gift of sensitivity and care that transcends the merely human. That natural inclination is a divine imprint that guides you to the ministry God has prepared for you.

Experiment and Evaluate

Don't be afraid to test your gift in different areas of ministry. Practice is essential to discovering and perfecting any spiritual ability. By getting involved in a variety of areas – whether it's in welcoming ministries, prayer teams, evangelistic campaigns, or any form of practical engagement – you'll be able to see where you feel most fulfillment, joy, and, most of all, impact. I have gone through seasons when I tried to serve in various ways, and as I evaluated, I learned that some areas accelerated my growth and fruit production, while others left me unsatisfied. This experimentation helps you to discover clearly where God has deposited your gift.

Listen to External Confirmation
Often, those who are close to us can see gifts in us that we ourselves do not recognize. Allow spiritual leaders and mature brethren to guide you and give you honest feedback. In my experience, I have received powerful confirmations from other believers who recognize in me the gift of teaching or exhortation, even though I would doubt its existence. This outward confirmation not only validates what Spirit has placed in you, but also strengthens your resolve to put it into action.

Evaluate yourself with Practical Tools
There are a variety of quizzes and spiritual resources available today that can help you identify your areas of strength. Use them with an attitude of prayer and humility, combining them with personal reflection and spiritual direction. These tools allow you to do honest self-analysis and detect patterns in your talents and in the community's response to your service.

Be Sensitive to the Fruit You Produce
The fruit of a true gift is visible. If what you do edifies, heals, comforts, or leads others to Jesus, it's a strong indicator that you're using your gift for God's glory. In my life, I have seen that when my service brings about positive change and transforms lives, that is the testimony of the fruit of the Spirit in

action. That visible blessing confirms to you that you are on the right path.

Persevere and Mature
Finally, it is vital to remember that gifts are not static; they develop and mature with use and time. What you see today is how a seed can grow into a leafy tree that gives shade and fruits in abundance. As in the parable of the talents (Matthew 25:14-30), use what you have and trust that by honoring God, He will multiply those gifts and allow you to grow in your ministry. Perseverance is key: stay immersed in the Lord's work, learn from every experience, and allow your gift to evolve in ways that make its impact ever more effective.

In this process of discovering and using your gifts, I invite you to ponder the following questions:

Questions for Personal Reflection:
1. Have you identified the spiritual gifts God has given you and feel His presence in your life?

2. In what concrete ways can you use your gifts to build up the Church and spread the gospel around you?

3. Do you allow the Holy Spirit to guide every area of your service, or do you sometimes

rely too much on your own skills and knowledge?

4. What steps can you take to prevent pride or competition from clouding the genuine purpose of your gift?

Questions for Community Discernment:
1. Is our Church promoting the use of spiritual gifts fairly and equitably among its members?

2. How can we help new believers discover, cultivate, and apply the gifts entrusted to them by the Holy Spirit?

3. Are we concentrating our efforts on allowing the Spirit's work to manifest freely, rather than getting stuck in organizational structures that limit our potential?

Each gift is a unique jewel that the Spirit places in us for a divine purpose. By discovering and putting into practice the gift God has entrusted to you, you not only fulfill your personal calling, but you also contribute to the edification and unity of the body of Christ, bearing witness to the transforming power of the gospel. May this meditation inspire you to embark on the exciting journey of discovering your spiritual gifts, and in doing so, to live a life of service filled with love and commitment to God's mission.

The Latter Rain: Unleashing the Gifts for the End Time!

May the Spirit guide you, strengthen you, and multiply your gift for the glory of God and the growth of His Church!

The Latter Rain: Unleashing the Gifts for the End Time!

Chapter 7: Developing Spiritual Gifts

I have experienced in my spiritual journey that the discovery of the gifts of the Spirit is only the beginning of a much deeper journey. Imagining that each gift is like a sacred seed that God has deposited within us fills me with wonder and hope. But, just as every seed needs to be cared for, nurtured, and exercised to bear fruit, our gifts demand dedication, discipline, and continued growth. I have learned that God has not called us to be passive servants but active co-workers in His work, and that every gift, when cultivated, becomes a powerful means of building up the body of Christ.

1. Biblical Principles on the Development of Gifts

The Bible teaches us that spiritual gifts are not static abilities, but living tools that must mature over time. I am reminded of Paul's exhortation in 2 Timothy 1:6: "Wherefore I put thee in remembrance that thou stir up the gift of God, which is in thee by the putting on of my hands."

This reminds me that, without exercise, our gifts can become inactive. God has endowed us with talents not only to know the truth, but to put it into practice in tangible ways. As 1 Peter 4:11 says, "¹ If any man speak, let him speak as the oracles of God; if any man minister, let him do it as of the ability which God giveth: that God in all things may be glorified through Jesus Christ, to whom be praise and dominion for ever and ever. Amen."

Believe, then, that every time you serve, every act of love and dedication in ministry is a step toward strengthening that gift. Paul also encourages us to use our gifts:

" Having then gifts differing according to the grace that is given to us, whether prophecy, let us prophesy according to the proportion of faith" (Romans 12:6).

These words have prompted me not to settle for a theoretical knowledge of my gift, but to practice it, to allow it to develop and to learn from each experience.

In addition, I have understood that spiritual growth requires humility and constant learning. Proverbs 27:17 tells us, " Iron sharpeneth iron; so a man sharpeneth the countenance of his friend."

This image has taught me that community of faith is critical to perfecting and polishing our gift. Friends and spiritual leaders, who wisely offer us correction and encouragement, are like that iron that sharpens iron.

2. Steps to Developing Spiritual Gifts

The development of a spiritual gift has become for me a process that involves several interconnected stages:

- **Exercise and Practice:** There is no substitute for practical action. I have learned to use my gift in different areas of service, facing times when, for fear of making mistakes, I doubted, but which I later understood were necessary lessons to grow. Every mistake was an opportunity to learn and refine my ability.

- **Training and Learning:** Studying God's Word has allowed me to deepen my calling. As I meditate on the biblical passages that deal with gifts — Romans 12, 1 Corinthians 12, Ephesians 4, and 1 Peter 4 — I have seen inspiring examples of how other believers put their gifts into action. In addition, seeking mentors and spiritual guides has been vital to better perfecting and understanding what God has entrusted to me.

- **Dependence on the Holy Spirit:** I have learned that praying constantly is essential to the growth of my gift. I ask the Lord to strengthen me, to direct every step, and to enable me to be an effective instrument in His work. It is in that dependence on the

Spirit that I find the confidence to act, knowing that I do not depend solely on my own abilities.

- **Evaluation and Growth:** Reflecting on the impact of my service has helped me adjust my approach. Asking myself if my actions have edified others and if my ministry has been faithful to God's direction serves as a compass. Community feedback and observation of visible fruits in the lives of others confirm to me that I am on the right path, or point me to areas for improvement.

3. Biblical Examples of Gift Development

The Bible is full of examples that have marked my heart. I remembered how **Moses**, despite his doubts and limitations, was called by God and progressively equipped to lead Israel (Exodus 3:10-12). I also reflected on **Samuel**, who in his youth learned to listen to the Lord's voice, developing a prophetic discernment that marked him for life (1 Samuel 3:1-10).

The apostle **Paul** is another powerful testimony. His transformation on the road to Damascus (Acts 9:15-20) and his subsequent dedication to teaching, which cemented fundamental doctrines of the Church, remind me that a gift, when cultivated with commitment and passion, can impact entire generations. Likewise, **Timothy** was activated and strengthened by the support of those who recognized in him the gift given by God (1 Timothy 4:14).

Historical and Cultural Context

Remembering the mindset of the Greco-Roman world helps me magnify the difference that biblical teaching makes. At that time, gifts were considered simply natural abilities or skills that could be acquired or perfected through training. However, the revelation of Scripture shows us that spiritual gifts are supernatural manifestations of the Holy Spirit, which require time and dedication to develop.

Today, the Church still faces similar challenges. Many people confuse human talent with divine gift, and at times, the fear of breaking comfort or passivity leads many to not exercise their gifts for the edification of the body of Christ. This disconnects from calling and mission prompts me to advocate for renewed engagement in the practice and development of our spiritual gifts.

God has entrusted every believer with talents and gifts, but it is our responsibility to cultivate them and use them for His glory. This reminds me that merely possessing a gift is not enough—it must be nurtured through prayer, deepened through study, and refined through dedication so that it may grow and bear fruit.

True success in God's work does not rest on human eloquence but on the presence of the Holy Spirit in every endeavor. These words inspire me to acknowledge my complete dependence on God and to continually seek the Spirit's guidance in all I do, knowing that without Him, my gift would remain mere words — void of transformative power.

As I conclude this meditation on the development of spiritual gifts, I pause to reflect and invite you to do the same:

Questions for Personal Reflection:
1. Have you identified the spiritual gifts God has given you and felt His call on your heart?

2. How can you strengthen and develop these gifts so that they are a source of edification for the Church?

3. Are you allowing the Holy Spirit to direct every area of your service, or do you sometimes lean too heavily on what you consider to be your own abilities?

4. What practical steps can you take to avoid passivity and ensure that your gift grows from a seed into a leafy tree of blessing?

Questions for Community Discernment:
1. Is our Church promoting the development of spiritual gifts in an equitable and practical way among all its members?

2. How can we help new believers discover and apply their gifts, so that the community benefits from the diversity that the Spirit offers?

3. Are we concentrating our efforts on the transforming work of the Holy Spirit, rather than getting caught up in organizational structures that stifle our potential?

Each gift is a sacred gift, a reflection of God's power and love in our lives, designed to be cultivated with intention and passion. By committing to the development of your gift, you not only grow in your personal service, but you also contribute to building a stronger, more vibrant, and continually expanding body of Christ. May this meditation inspire you to embrace every step in the process of developing your gifts, to persevere, and to allow the Holy Spirit to multiply and transform every action for the glory of God and the growth of His Church. May the Lord lead you, refresh your spirit, and empower you mightily at every step of this incredible spiritual journey!

How can we make sure we are using our gifts for the glory of God and the growth of His Church?

In my daily walk with Christ, I have experienced that our gifts are not mere abilities to show off, but sacred gifts that the Holy Spirit entrusts to us to transform lives. Over time I have learned that to ensure that we are using these gifts for the glory of God and the growth of His Church, it is necessary to cultivate a life of faithfulness, excellence, and humility. I want to share with you some truths that have guided my own ministry and that, I hope, will inspire you to put into practice what God has placed in you.

1. Use Your Gift Faithfully

I remember well the parable of the talents in Matthew 25:14-30: Jesus taught us that gifts multiply by using them. Like a sower who does not water his seed, a gift that is not put into action withers and loses its potential. From my first steps in service, I learned that there is no need to wait until I feel "fully ready" to start using my gift. Rather, I acted on what I had, trusting that each experience would shape me and strengthen my calling. This conviction has led me to see that every act of service, no matter how small it may seem, is a testimony of God's power transforming itself in us for the benefit of His kingdom.

2. Train with Excellence

Although our gifts come from the Spirit, I have found that they also require training, study, and practice. If God has endowed me with the gift of teaching, I have committed myself to immerse myself in the Word and to study pedagogical methodologies in order to communicate the truth clearly. I have found that in every book of the Bible and in every spiritual reflection, I discover tools that sharpen my ability to lead others. It is a path of continuous growth in which diligent effort is honored and multiplied, because God appreciates a committed heart.

3. Seek Spiritual Mentors

There are times when I have felt insecure about my gift, and it has been in those moments that the wisdom of mature leaders and brethren has been invaluable. Surround yourself, as I did, with those who have cultivated their own gifts and humbly share their experience. Listening to their advice, seeing their example, and sharing my progress has allowed me to grow in discernment and clarity. Trust that the body of Christ is a community of love and discernment, where every word and every look shares God's truth in the midst of darkness.

4. Ask for Continual Filling of the Spirit

I have learned that the development of gifts does not depend on human techniques, but on a daily life filled with the Holy Spirit. It is through constant prayer, Bible study, fasting, and obedience that we open doors for the Spirit to refine our ability to serve. I feel the difference of a constant communion with the Lord: that intentionality has transformed me and allowed me to experience a fullness that surpasses any human expectation, reminding me that without God's presence, our gifts lack their true power.

5. Evaluate your fruit constantly

Every once in a while, I stop to reflect on how my gift has impacted the community. Have I built the faith of those around me? Have I glorified the Lord by my actions? Evaluating the fruit of our ministry is crucial, for what we give to others should be a reflection of God's love. In my experience, seeing the joy and transformation in the lives of others has been the greatest confirmation that I am on the right path. Do not hesitate to adjust your focus, always with humility and prayer, when you feel that it is necessary to grow or change.

6. Accept Correction with Maturity

Throughout this journey, I have understood that growing in our gift also means being willing to receive corrections and advice. Every servant who grows needs to be molded, and I have learned to appreciate sincere feedback from those who have pointed out areas for improvement. Correction, when it comes from a place of love and for the purpose of edifying each other, is a precious gift. Remember that your character and holy living are the best channels for the Spirit to work in you.

7. Stay Humble

Never forget that the gift you possess is not something you have earned on your own merit, but a gift from the Spirit. The true strength of your ministry lies in your total surrender to God. As 1 Corinthians 1:31 says, "Let him who boasts, boast in the Lord." This humility frees you and allows you to be a more effective tool, as you recognize that all power and efficacy come from the grace of the Creator.

8. Multiply What You Have Received in Others

Maturity in the use of a gift is not measured only by what one has personally developed, but also by the ability to empower and encourage others. When I reached a point where my gift had matured, I discovered the joy of forming disciples, of sharing what I had learned, and of seeing the gifts God had placed in them awakened in others. Multiplying what you have received is the path to vibrant and expansive ministry. Teaching and training others not only build up the Church but also strengthens unity and the advancement of the gospel.

I invite you to stop and meditate on these questions in your personal life:

1. Have you identified the spiritual gifts God has given you and feel His call in your heart?

2. How can you begin today to use your gifts, even with what you have, to flourish in service?

3. Are you cultivating a daily relationship with the Holy Spirit that allows you to grow in your gift, or are you leaning into your own abilities without seeking divine filling?

4. What concrete steps can you take to avoid pride and passivity, and instead maintain an attitude of constant learning and growth?

And in community, let us reflect together:

1. Is our Church actively promoting the development of spiritual gifts in each of its members?

2. How can we help new believers discover and apply their gifts in a way that builds up the whole community?

3. Are we prioritizing the active ministry and work of the Holy Spirit over rigid structures that limit the potential for service?

Each gift is a jewel that the Spirit has placed in our hands for an eternal purpose. By developing our capacities and putting into practice what God has entrusted to us, we not only grow personally, but we contribute to the flourishing of a stronger, more united, and ever-expanding body of Christ. May this reflection inspire you to embrace the development of your gifts with passion, dedication, and a humble dependence on the Spirit, so that all that you do will glorify God and build up His Church. May the Lord guide you through every step of this wonderful process!

Chapter 8: The Discovery of Spiritual Gifts

A Call to Do God's Will
From the moment we give our lives to Christ, the Holy Spirit seals us with His presence and equips us with spiritual gifts. These gifts are not mere human talents or abilities, but supernatural manifestations that enable us to serve in the Kingdom of God.

However, there is a responsibility that falls on every believer: to discover what gift or gifts have been imparted to him at the time of his baptism. It is not enough to receive them; we must activate them, develop them, and use them for the glory of God and the growth of His Church.

Romans 12:2 exhorts us, " And be not conformed to this world: but be ye transformed by the renewing of your mind, that ye may prove what is that good, and acceptable, and perfect, will of God."

When we discover our spiritual gift and use it according to God's purpose, we enter into the fullness of God's will, which is good, pleasing, and perfect.

Baptism: The Starting Point

Baptism is not just a symbolic act; It is a time of spiritual transformation. It is the instant when the believer publicly declares his faith and receives the impartation of the Holy Spirit.

At that time, God deposits in us specific gifts that enable us to fulfill His purpose. Not everyone receives the same gift, but each receives what is necessary to build up the body of Christ.

If you have been baptized into Christ, you already have a gift. The question is: have you discovered it?

The Responsibility to Discover Our Gifts

God does not force us to use our gifts; it invites us to discover them and put them into action.

Many believers live without knowing the potential that God has placed in them. Some doubt they have a gift, others are afraid to use it, and others simply don't know how to identify it.

But Scripture calls us to renew our understanding, to seek God's will, and to live to the fullest. Discovering our gift is part of that process of transformation.

The Latter Rain: Unleashing the Gifts for the End Time!

Steps to Discover and Activate Our Spiritual Gifts

If you want to know the gift God has given you, here are some key steps that can help you in this process:

1. Pray with Expectation: Prayer is the first step in discovering our gifts. Ask the Holy Ghost to reveal to you how He has equipped you to serve.

    James 1:5 tells us, "If any of you lacks wisdom, let him ask of God, who gives to all abundantly." God does not hide His will; He wants you to know your purpose.

2. Study God's Word: Spiritual gifts are clearly described in the Bible. Take time to read passages like Romans 12, 1 Corinthians 12, Ephesians 4, and 1 Peter 4.

    As you study the Word, God will open your understanding and show you how the gifts have operated in the history of the Church.

3. Reflect on Your Passion and Effectiveness: God often aligns our gifts with our natural inclinations. Think about the areas where you feel a deep passion and where you have seen fruit in your service.

    If you enjoy teaching and people are edified by your words, you may have the gift of teaching. If you feel a burden from interceding in prayer and see supernatural responses, you may have the gift of intercession.

4. Seek Confirmation in the Community: Often, other believers can see in us gifts that we ourselves do not recognize. Listen to feedback from spiritual leaders and mature brethren.

   If several people have told you that you have a specific gift, chances are God is confirming His calling on your life.

5. Experiment and Evaluate: Don't be afraid to try different service areas. Practice is essential to discovering and perfecting any spiritual ability.

   Serve in different ministries and see where you feel most fulfilled and where you see the most impact. God will guide you to the place where your gift blossoms.

6. Be Sensitive to the Fruit You Produce: The fruit of a true gift is visible. If what you do edifies, heals, comforts, or leads others to Jesus, it's a strong indicator that you're using your gift for God's glory. Jesus said in Matthew 7:16, "By their fruits you will know them."

   If your service is producing spiritual fruit, it is a sign that you are walking in your calling.

7. Persevere and Mature in Your Gift: Gifts are not static; they develop and mature over time. As in

the parable of the talents (Matthew 25:14-30), use what God has given you and trust that He will multiply it.

Fulfilling God's Will
When we discover our gift and use it for God's glory, we enter into the fullness of His will.

There is no greater satisfaction than knowing that we are walking in divine purpose, building up the Church, and glorifying our heavenly Father.

If you haven't identified your gift yet, today is the day to begin that process.

Pray, study, reflect, seek confirmation, experience, and observe the fruit. God has equipped you with something special. Don't keep it, use it for His glory.

May the Holy Spirit guide you on this beautiful journey of discovery and activation of your gifts. May your life be a living witness to God's will, good, pleasing and perfect.

Questionnaire I

to discover spiritual gifts

The first step in discovering spiritual gifts is to take an overview of all the gifts and see which one of them catches your eye and which one or which of them you think you have. The following

The Latter Rain: Unleashing the Gifts for the End Time!

questionnaire may be of help to achieve that purpose.

Answer *Yes*, if you think you have that gift; *No*, if you think you don't; *Perhaps*, if you believe that there is any chance that this gift is the one that the Holy Spirit has bestowed upon you.

Gifts	Yes	No	Maybe
Prophecy	___	___	___
Service	___	___	___
Teaching	___	___	___
Exhortation	___	___	___
Gifts	___	___	___
Leadership	___	___	___
Mercy	___	___	___
Wisdom	___	___	___
Knowledge	___	___	___
Faith	___	___	___
Healthcare	___	___	___
Miracles	___	___	___
Discernment	___	___	___
Languages	___	___	___
Interpretation	___	___	___
Apostleship	___	___	___
Aid	___	___	___

Gifts	Yes	No	Maybe
Administration	___	___	___
Evangelism	___	___	___
Pastorate	___	___	___
Celibacy	___	___	___
Hospitality	___	___	___
Missionary	___	___	___
Intercession	___	___	___
Exorcism	___	___	___

Table I

Next, write down all the gifts to which I answer Yes or Maybe. Read them several times. Pray that God will clearly indicate to you if these are your spiritual gifts.

Discovering Our Spiritual Gifts: A Journey of Revelation and Purpose

The Holy Spirit has bestowed spiritual gifts upon every believer, but discovering and activating them is a personal and spiritual responsibility. It is not an automatic process or a knowledge that simply appears; it is a journey of searching, prayer, and confirmation.

Each gift is a divine tool designed to build up the body of Christ and glorify God. They are not natural talents or acquired abilities, but supernatural manifestations that enable us to serve in the Kingdom.

If today you are wondering how to discover your spiritual gift, I invite you to walk this path with faith and expectation. God desires to reveal to you the purpose He has placed in you.

1. The New Birth: The Gateway

Spiritual gifts are exclusively for members of the body of Christ. Whoever is not born again has no spiritual gifts, because these are imparted by the Holy Spirit to the children of God.

Jesus said in John 3:5, "*Unless one is born of water and of the Spirit, he cannot enter the kingdom of God.*"

If you haven't yet had a personal encounter with Christ, the first step is not to discover your gift, but to give your life to Him. Only those who have been regenerated by the Holy Spirit receive the impartation of gifts to serve in the Kingdom.

If you have already been born again, then you can move forward in this process of discovery.

2. Believe in Spiritual Gifts

Many believers live without activating their gifts because they don't believe God has given them one.

However, the Bible assures us in 1 Corinthians 12:7: *"But to each one is given the manifestation of the Spirit for profit."*

God excludes no one. If you are part of the body of Christ, you have at least one spiritual gift.

Believing in this truth is fundamental. God has equipped you with something special for His glory.

3. Pray for Help to Discover the Gifts
The Holy Ghost is the giver of gifts, and He wants you to discover them. If you ask Him in prayer sincerely, He will guide you.

James 1:5 tells us, *"If any of you lacks wisdom, let him ask of God, who gives to all abundantly."*

Make time for prayer, asking for revelation about your gift. God will answer.

4. Study About Spiritual Gifts
To discover the gifts, it is necessary to know them. Spend time reading passages such as:

- Romans 12
- 1 Corinthians 12
- Ephesians 4

- 1 Peter 4

You can also study books and teachings by Christian authors who have delved into this topic. The more knowledge you have, the clearer you will be about your calling.

5. Special attention to each gift
Don't limit yourself to the most visible or popular gifts. Every gift is precious and necessary in the body of Christ.

Take time to study each of the spiritual gifts and their characteristics. God may have given you a gift that you didn't expect, but that is key to His work.

6. Reflect on Your Natural Inclination
After studying the gifts, ask yourself which ones appeal to you the most.

Do you feel a special inclination towards any ministry?

Are you passionate about teaching, serving, exhorting, interceding?

Are there areas where you feel naturally effective?

God often aligns our gifts with our spiritual inclinations. Listen to that inner voice that guides you.

7. Experience the Gifts

It is not enough to reflect; it is necessary to put the gifts into practice.

If you're inclined to teach, try sharing a Bible study. If you think you have the gift of service, get involved in helping activities.

Experimentation is key to confirming your call. Don't be afraid to try different areas of ministry.

8. Evaluate Satisfaction in Ministering the Gift

When you minister a gift, you should feel joy and fulfillment.

Jesus said in John 15:11, "*These things I have spoken to you, that my joy may be in you, and your joy may be full.*"

If you feel peace, joy, and satisfaction when you exercise a gift, it is a sign that God has called you to that area.

If you don't feel joy, that may not be your gift, and you need to keep exploring.

9. Identify Ability in the Exercise of the Gift
Spiritual gifts not only bring satisfaction, but they also come with skill.

If you have a gift, you will exercise it easily and effectively.

If something costs you too much and you don't see fruit, it may not be your gift.

10. Confirmation by the Body of Christ
External confirmation is key. If your community recognizes your gift and is built up by it, it is a sign that God has called you to that area.

If several people have told you that you have a specific gift, chances are God is confirming His purpose in your life.

11. Evaluate Impact and Blessing
The purpose of the gifts is to build up the Church. If your service is producing growth, healing, and transformation in others, it is a sign that you are walking in your calling.

Jesus said in Matthew 7:16, "*By their fruits you will know them.*"

If you see fruit in your ministry, it is a confirmation that you are using your gift correctly.

12. Final Step: Pray and Ask for Confirmation Regularly

The discovery of gifts is not a single event, but an ongoing process.

Pray each year for direction. Ask your pastor or spiritual mentor to help you assess your growth.

God can add new gifts to your life over time. Be open to His guidance.

Conclusion: A Call to Activate Your Gift

God has equipped you with a special gift. Don't keep it, use it for His glory.

If you haven't figured it out yet, today is the day to start that process.

Pray, study, reflect, experiment, and observe the fruit.

May the Holy Spirit guide you on this beautiful journey of discovery and activation of your gifts. May your life be a living testimony of God's power in action.

The Path to the Discovery of Spiritual Gifts

Discovering the spiritual gift that God has placed in us is a journey that goes beyond a simple test or a personal evaluation. It is a process of divine revelation, ministry growth, and confirmation within the body of Christ.

This quiz is just an introductory guide, a starting point for exploring the calling God has placed on your life. However, spiritual discernment, ministry experience, and community confirmation are essential to fully knowing your gift.

The Holy Spirit not only bestows gifts, but also guides us in their discovery and development. As we serve, pray, and seek direction, we begin to see clearly how God has equipped us for His work.

Ministry experience allows us to test and perfect our gifts. It is not enough to identify them; We must exercise them, allow them to ripen, and observe the fruit they bear in the lives of others.

Community confirmation is key. God does not call us to isolation, but to mutual edification within His Church. Often, fellow believers can see in us gifts that we have not yet recognized. Hearing the voice of the community and receiving their affirmation helps us walk safely in our calling.

Therefore, this process should not be taken lightly. It is not only an intellectual exercise, but a deep spiritual search.

The Latter Rain: Unleashing the Gifts for the End Time!

If you ask yourself today what your gift is, open your heart to the guidance of the Holy Spirit. Pray, serve, listen, and allow God to reveal His purpose in your life.

The discovery of your gift is not the ultimate destination, but the beginning of a life of service and growth in the Kingdom of God. May this path lead you to greater intimacy with the Lord and a meaningful contribution to His Church.

May the Holy Spirit illuminate your path and confirm in you the call he has placed on your life!

Questionnaire II

The following questionnaire can be very helpful in discovering the spiritual gifts that God has granted. Based on tools adapted from C. Peter Wagner, William McRae and Rick Yohn.

Mark
0 If the answer is **completely false**
1 If the answer is **mostly false**
2 Whether the answer is partially false or true
3 If the answer is **Mostly true**
4 If the answer is completely true

It is very important that you answer each question

1. 0 1 2 3 4   Do you like to talk to people and present God's will for them?

2. 0 1 2 3 4   Do you feel joy when you are asked to do special crafts in your Church?

3. 0 1 2 3 4   Do you understand the biblical doctrines of the Church in detail?

4. 0 1 2 3 4   Do you feel able to comfort someone who is perplexed or suffering?

5. 0 1 2 3 4   Do you manage your money well in such a way that you can give freely to God's cause?

6. 0 1 2 3 4   Do you enjoy being among people and participating in their activities?

7. 0 1 2 3 4   Do you sympathize with and try to help drug addicts, the evicted, people on the street, etc.?

8. 0 1 2 3 4   Do you easily discover new biblical truths for yourself?

9. 0 1 2 3 4   Is it easy for you to choose between the various biblical alternatives for solving complicated problems in the Church?

10. 0 1 2 3 4   Do you firmly believe in God's promises?

11. 0 1 2 3 4   Do you sympathize with those who suffer from illness?

12. 0 1 2 3 4   Does God answer your prayers in special, sometimes supernatural, ways?

13. 0 1 2 3 4   Do you clearly perceive the difference between truth and error?

14. 0 1 2 3 4   Have you secretly prayed in some language unknown to you?

15. 0 1 2 3 4   Have you stated in your own language any message that has been given in a language unknown to you?

16. 0 1 2 3 4   Do you feel called by God to be responsible for the care and leadership of God's people?

17. 0 1 2 3 4   Do you enjoy helping Church leaders so that they can devote more time to matters essential to the Church?

18. 0 1 2 3 4   Do you enjoy solving complicated problems in the Church?

19. 0 1 2 3 4   Do you feel joy in sharing God's Word with others?

20. 0 1 2 3 4   Do you like the idea of visiting the brethren of the Church regularly?

21. 0 1 2 3 4   Do you like the idea of staying unmarried to devote all your time to the Church?

22. 0 1 2 3 4   Are you interested in searching and finding people who don't have food or accommodation?

23. 0 1 2 3 4   Does it adapt easily to other cultures?

24. 0 1 2 3 4   Do you lose track of time when you pray?

25. 0 1 2 3 4   Do you think your faith is strong enough to be able to cast the devil out of some possessed person?

26. 0 1 2 3 4   Do you feel you can encourage and strengthen the discouraged?

27. 0 1 2 3 4   Do you enjoy participating in the order and cleanliness of the Church?

28. 0 1 2 3 4   Do you enjoy reading Bible commentaries and poring over difficult passages in the Bible?

29. 0 1 2 3 4   Do people look to you for advice about their problems?

30. 1 2 3 4 Do you give objects or money to the Church very liberally?

31. 0 1 2 3 4   Do you enjoy planning and carrying out activities for the Church?

32. 0 1 2 3 4   Are you sensitive to the needs of the elderly and disabled and seek to help them in some way?

33. 0 1 2 3 4   Do you enjoy seeking solutions to complicated problems in the Church?

34. 0 1 2 3 4   Do you study or read enough to learn Bible truths?

35. 0 1 2 3 4   Do you read the Bible and pray several times every day?

36. 0 1 2 3 4   Do you feel inclined to pray for the sick?

The Latter Rain: Unleashing the Gifts for the End Time!

37. 0 1 2 3 4   Do you believe that in the name of God, through faith and prayer, you are able to alter the natural order of things?

38. 0 1 2 3 4   Can you discern the motives that move people?

39. 0 1 2 3 4   Have you felt the need to give a message to the Church in a language unknown to you?

40. 0 1 2 3 4   Have you experienced understanding a language that you have never studied before?

41. 0 1 2 3 4   Are you able to start a group of believers or consolidate an existing group?

42. 0 1 2 3 4   Do you enjoy helping out in the pastor's office?

43. **4 0 1 2 3 4**   Can you accurately predict the outcome of your decisions?

44. 0 1 2 3 4   Are you comfortable asking someone to accept Jesus as their savior?

45. 0 1 2 3 4   Do you think you would like to visit Church interests and study the Bible with them?

46. 0 1 2 3 4   Is it easy for you to think about not living the rest of your life in intimacy with someone of the opposite sex?

47. 0 1 2 3 4   Are you happy when someone visits you and asks you to stay at home for a few days?

48. 0 1 2 3 4   Do you feel comfortable among people of another race or nationality?

49. 0 1 2 3 4   Do you take prayer requests very seriously and pray for them in your home?

50. 0 1 2 3 4   Are you not afraid of the idea of being face to face with a demoniac?

51. 0 1 2 3 4   Has he admonished others by producing correction and repentance?

52. 0 1 2 3 4   Do you feel satisfaction in doing housework in God's house?

53. 0 1 2 3 4   Do you enjoy sharing your discoveries or understanding of God's Word with others?

54. 0 1 2 3 4   Do you find it easy to apply biblical principles to problems in the Church?

55. 0 1 2 3 4   Do you like to encourage others to give money liberally to the Church?

56. 0 1 2 3 4   Are you comfortable delegating responsibilities to others?

57. 0 1 2 3 4   Would you like to belong to a visitation group for the incarcerated?

58. 0 1 2 3 4   Do you find it easy to understand Bible truths that are difficult for others?

59. 0 1 2 3 4   Do you feel confident that you know God's will for the progress of the Church?

60. 0 1 2 3 4   Do you fully trust God's power during difficult situations?

61. 0 1 2 3 4   Do you think you can heal the sick in the name of God?

62. 0 1 2 3 4   Do you think God can use it to perform supernatural acts?

63. 0 1 2 3 4   Do you know when a person is influenced by God or the devil?

64. 0 1 2 3 4   Have you spoken in any unknown languages?

65. 0 1 2 3 4   Would you like to be able to interpret a message given in an unknown language?

66. 0 1 2 3 4   Are you consulted by other brethren as to ecclesiastical or doctrinal problems?

67. 0 1 2 3 4   Do you care for those in need and seek to help them?

68. 0 1 2 3 4   Do you feel skilled at developing plans and bringing them to fruition?

69. 0 1 2 3 4   Do you prefer to spend your free time sharing the gospel with others?

70. 0 1 2 3 4   Do you like the idea of having to preach at church every week?

71. 0 1 2 3 4   Do you think you wouldn't miss out on any blessings if you stay unmarried?

72. 0 1 2 3 4   Is "my house is your home" your favorite saying and do you practice it constantly?

73. 0 1 2 3 4   Would you enjoy life living in a foreign country?

74. 0 1 2 3 4   Do you like to pray for the Church constantly?

75. 0 1 2 3 4   Do you like the idea of being able to confront the devil face to face and be able to dominate him in the name of Jesus?

76. 0 1 2 3 4   Have you been impressed with special messages that you make known regardless of the consequences?

77. 0 1 2 3 4   Are you comfortable obeying orders rather than giving them?

78. 0 1 2 3 4   Do you feel able to explain Bible teachings clearly to others?

79. 0 1 2 3 4   Do you like to encourage the fickle and discouraged?

80. 0 1 2 3 4   Do you feel moved and try to do something when the Church needs financial help?

81. 0 1 2 3 4   Do you feel that your influence affects others positively to work for the Lord?

82. 0 1 2 3 4   Do you find it very difficult to miss a beggar?

83. 0 1 2 3 4   Do you find it easy to present alternatives to problems without having to take sides?

84. 0 1 2 3 4   Do you think you have complete mastery of Bible truths?

85. 0 1 2 3 4   Are you not usually discouraged when things are not going well in the Church?

86. 0 1 2 3 4   Do you pray so much for the sick that they feel healed?

87. 0 1 2 3 4   Have you performed any miracles by the power of God?

88. 0 1 2 3 4   Can you recognize spiritual gifts in others?

89. 0 1 2 3 4   Does the idea of being able to speak in tongues appeal to you?

90. 0 1 2 3 4   Do you think that the gifts of tongues and interpretation are really necessary in these days for the proclamation of the Gospel?

91. 0 1 2 3 4   Are their opinions taken seriously and followed by the rest of the brethren in the Church?

92. 0 1 2 3 4   Do you enjoy going and distributing literature, magazines, and brochures?

93. 0 1 2 3 4   Do you prefer to preside over meetings and plot targets rather than just be a participant?

94. 0 1 2 3 4   Do you feel the desire to talk to unbelievers in order to win them to Christ?

95. 0 1 2 3 4   Are you excited about the idea of being able to be the pastor of your church?

96. 0 1 2 3 4   Do you think that if you were to marry, your family would be a hindrance to your ministry rather than a blessing?

97. 0 1 2 3 4   Do you like to greet Church visitors and invite them to eat or even sleep in your home if necessary?

98. 0 1 2 3 4   Do you feel the need to be a preacher in other countries?

99. 0 1 2 3 4   Is prayer your favorite spiritual exercise?

100.   0 1 2 3 4   Have you ever used God's power to cast the devil out of someone?

101.   0 1 2 3 4   Is the overall progress of the body of Christ and the satisfaction of the needs of the brethren an obsession in your life?

102.   0 1 2 3 4   Do you feel a lot of joy and satisfaction when you can serve someone?

103.   0 1 2 3 4   Do you enjoy teaching about the Bible and feel that your students are practicing its teachings?

104.   0 1 2 3 4   Do you feel a strong desire to call attention to those who are doing wrong?

105.   0 1 2 3 4   Are you able to raise large amounts of money for the Lord's cause?

106. 0 1 2 3 4   Do you feel able to recruit other brothers and put them to work for the Church?

107.   1 2 3 4 Do you easily go the second mile and turn the other cheek?

108. 0 1 2 3 4   Do other leaders and leaders usually seek his counsel and make them clearly understand his plans which prove to be a blessing to the Church?

109. 0 1 2 3 4   Are you sought out by the other brothers to answer their questions and concerns?

110. 0 1 2 3 4   Of the Christian graces, is faith one of your favorites?

111. 0 1 2 3 4   Do you care about the physical health of your fellow human beings and feel a desire to do something about it?

112. 0 1 2 3 4   Have you ever felt the desire and strong inclination to ask God to perform some supernatural act for the benefit of another, believing that God will answer your request?

113. 0 1 2 3 4   Do you perceive the presence of evil before it becomes apparent?

114. 0 1 2 3 4   Do you think that the gift of tongues is necessary today for the building up of the body of Christ?

115.   0 1 2 3 4   Do you think it is necessary and beneficial for the Church to provide messages in unknown languages and interpret them?

116.   0 1 2 3 4   Have you felt it your duty to call out some Church administrator or leader who is not doing well?

117.   0 1 2 3 4   Do you like the idea of being a Bible teacher?

118.   0 1 2 3 4   Do you feel qualified to preside over or oversee the rest of the fellowship of the Church?

119.   0 1 2 3 4   Do you clearly understand the steps that lead a person to salvation?

120.   0 1 2 3 4   Would you like to organize, plan, and oversee all Church activities?

121.   0 1 2 3 4   Do you consider yourself capable of staying unmarried without the fear of "burning"?

122.   0 1 2 3 4   Do you regularly have guests at your table and home?

123.   0 1 2 3 4   Doesn't it bother you to be separated from your family for long periods of time, or forever, in order to preach the gospel in other lands?

The Latter Rain: Unleashing the Gifts for the End Time!

124.   0 1 2 3 4   Does God answer your prayers frequently and in a tangible way?

125.   0 1 2 3 4   Are you lured into situations where there are demon-possessed people and are you sought out to cast out the demon because of your use of God's power?

Evaluation

In the table below, the number in each box represents the quiz question.

- Write down the numbers 0 through 4 in each box according to what you answered in each question.
- Add up the values you gave in each box in the horizontal columns.
- Place the amount under the box that says total. That is, add the value you gave to questions 1, 26, 76, 101 and so on.

Table II

Total Gifts

1	26	51	76	101	=	Prophecy
2	27	52	77	102	=	Service
3	28	53	78	103	=	Teaching
4	29	54	79	104	=	Exhortation
5	30	55	80	105	=	Gifts
6	31	56	81	106	=	Leadership
7	32	57	82	107	=	Mercy
8	33	58	83	108	=	Wisdom
9	34	59	84	109	=	Knowledge
10	35	60	85	110	=	Faith
11	36	61	86	111	=	Healthcare
12	37	62	87	112	=	Miracles
13	38	63	88	113	=	Discernment
14	39	64	89	114	=	Languages
15	40	65	90	115	=	Interpretation
16	41	66	91	116	=	Apostleship
17	42	67	92	117	=	Aid
18	43	68	93	118	=	Administration
19	44	69	94	119	=	Evangelism
20	45	70	95	120	=	Pastorate
21	46	71	96	121	=	Celibacy
22	47	72	97	122	=	Hospitality
23	48	73	98	123	=	Missionary
24	49	74	99	124	=	Intercession
25	50	75	100	125	=	Exorcism

The Latter Rain: Unleashing the Gifts for the End Time!

Results

Circulate the highest numbers in the totals table and place these gifts in the next column:

1. _____
2. _____
3. _____
4. _____
5. _____

Compare this list with Table I.

Which gifts from Table I that you answered "Yes" are listed above?

1. _____
2. _____
3. _____
4. _____

Now write down the gifts that, although not in any of the above tables or lists, you think have been conferred on you by the Holy Spirit:

1. _____
2. _____

3. _____

4. _____

5. _____

Confirmation and Purpose: Acknowledging the Gift God Has Bestowed on You

The results you have obtained are not mere coincidences or simple indicators. They are a window into the work that the Holy Spirit is already doing in your life. Although these results point to areas of high possibility, there is a good chance that these are some of the gifts the Lord has bestowed upon you for the advancement and advancement of the body of Christ.

God does not give gifts at random. Every spiritual ability He places in His children has a divine purpose: to build His Church, strengthen His people, and extend His Kingdom. If you feel an inclination toward certain gifts today, don't ignore it. The Holy Ghost may be confirming His call on your life.

This is a moment of reflection and action. It is not enough to recognize the gift; it needs to be activated, developed and used faithfully. God has equipped you with something special, and the body of Christ needs what He has put in you.

The Latter Rain: Unleashing the Gifts for the End Time!

Are you ready to walk in your purpose? Pray, seek direction, and allow the Holy Spirit to guide you in this process. Your gift isn't just for you; it is for the glory of God and the building up of His Church.

May the Lord strengthen and confirm you in His calling!

Epilogue: Prepared for the Latter Rain

This book addresses the profound theme of spiritual gifts, their discovery, development, and their importance for the mission of the Church in recent times. To strengthen this work with research and scholarly sources, it is helpful to support the topics covered with theological and psychological studies that delve into spiritual gifts from a historical, biblical, and practical perspective. Here are some key areas that can be bolstered with research:

1. Spiritual Gifts: A Theological Basis

Theological Research: Cite studies such as "*Showing the Spirit: A Theological Exposition of 1 Corinthians 12-14*" by D.A. Carson, which addresses the role of spiritual gifts within the body of Christ, and how they contribute to the unity and mission of the Church.

Biblical and Historical Context: In addition to the passages from 1 Corinthians 12, one could include **Gordon D. Fee's work** in "*Paul, the Spirit, and the People of God,*" which exposes how Paul views spiritual gifts not only as abilities, but as manifestations of God's power.

2. The Latter Rain and Eschatology

Eschatological Theology: References to the "latter rain" and the outpouring of the Holy Spirit are deeply connected to Christian eschatology. The concept can be enriched by studies such as those of **William McRae**, who explores the dynamics of ministry and the action of the Spirit in the end times, emphasizing their relationship to the global mission of the Church.

The Impact of the Spirit on Revival: This theme can be strengthened by reflections on revival and spiritual gifts in the work of Ellen G. White, such as in "*The Great Controversy*" and "*The Way to Christ*," which underscores the spiritual preparation of the Church before the Second Coming of Christ.

3. Developing Spiritual Gifts in the Community

Discernment and Spiritual Growth: The importance of discernment and the evolution of spiritual gifts within the community can be supported by Rick **Yohn's work** in "*Discover your spiritual gift and use it*," which focuses on the practical evaluation of spiritual gifts in the context of community and church life.

Formation and Training: In addition, it can refer to research on how practical use and training in spiritual gifts are fundamental to church growth, as addressed in "*The Dynamics of Spiritual Gifts*" by William McRae.

4. The Union and Diversity of the Body of Christ

Theology of Unity in Diversity: Principles about interdependence in the body of Christ can be supported by research on how the unity and diversity of the Church reinforce its overall mission, drawing on the teachings of **John Stott** in *"The Authentic Church,"* where he highlights the value of ecclesiastical unity in the multiplication of gifts.

Practical and Psychological Dimension: From a more applied perspective, Christian organizational psychology can provide insights on how to foster unity and collaborative use of gifts within the community, as explained by **C. Peter Wagner** in *"Your spiritual gifts can help your church grow,"* which relates the effective use of gifts to the growth and health of the church.

5. The Role of the Church in Activating the Gifts

Early Church Practices: Biblical references and historical practices of the early church, such as those described in **Acts of the Apostles**, can support an understanding of the essential role of the Church in activating and using spiritual gifts. The apostolic model can offer practical examples of how these gifts are operative in times of crisis and need, aligned with the mission of the Church.

The promise still echoes in prophecy: God will pour out His Spirit on all flesh. The latter rain is about to fall, and those who have discovered, developed, and dedicated their gifts to the cause of the gospel will be like torches lit in the midst of darkness.

This book is not written to inform, but to ignite. It does not seek to fill your mind only, but to mobilize your soul. Because spiritual gifts are a call to service, to action, to complete dedication for the love of Christ.

As the world shakes in crises, wars, deception and spiritual coldness, the Church is called to shine as never before. Every gift, no matter how small it may seem, has a place in God's eternal plan. He did not save you so that you would remain passive, but so that you would be an instrument of salvation for others.

Today is the time to consecrate yourself. Today is the day to say, "Lord, here I am. Fill me, use me, transform me." If the seed of this book has fallen on fertile soil, trust that the Spirit will bring growth, power, fruit. and fire from heaven.

May the breath of the Spirit lift up a generation of believers anointed, courageous, and filled with the love of Christ. And may the Church of the living God, adorned with the gifts of the Spirit, proclaim with power the last good news before the glorious return of our Savior.

The rain is about to fall.
We are called to receive it. Amen.

Meet The Author

Dr. Mariangeli Morauske is a distinguished leader whose multifaceted career spans academia, spiritual guidance, and transformational writing. Driven by an unwavering dedication to education and service, she has held diverse roles including teacher, principal, academic dean, and chaplain—each one reflecting her commitment to excellence and compassion.

As an author of more than ten books, Dr. Morauske addresses foundational themes such as courtship, marriage, family restoration, theology, and holistic health. Her work offers both practical strategies and spiritual insight, empowering individuals to pursue healing and purpose from a faith-based perspective. Her writings not only inform but transform, blending theological depth with accessible wisdom.

In the classroom, Dr. Morauske is known for her dynamic teaching style and profound knowledge. Her innovative approach to education has inspired countless students and earned her widespread respect across academic communities. As a chaplain, she extends her ministry beyond the lecture hall, offering heartfelt spiritual support to those navigating life's challenges—always rooted in empathy and unwavering faith.

The Latter Rain: Unleashing the Gifts for the End Time!

At home, Dr. Morauske is a loving wife to her husband, Daniel, and a devoted mother to two accomplished children. Her daughter, Leilani, serves as a registered nurse and clinical educator on the Navajo Indian reservation in Arizona. Her son, Josiah, is an IT specialist in Fort Worth, Texas. Balancing professional and personal responsibilities with grace, Dr. Morauske exemplifies resilience and deep care.

Her academic credentials include a Master's in Counseling Psychology from National University, a Master's in Pastoral Ministry from Andrews University, and a Doctor of Medicine—underscoring her holistic approach to human well-being.

Her life's path has led her across the globe, including years spent in Israel, Puerto Rico, Venezuela, Colombia, Mexico, and now Texas. These global experiences have enriched her worldview and deepened her cross-cultural ministry. Above all, Dr. Morauske lives as a servant of God, devoted to a life of purpose, love, and unwavering faith.

The Latter Rain: Unleashing the Gifts for the End Time!

Bibliography

Biblia Reina Valera 1960. (1960). *Holy Bible*. United Bible Societies.

Blackaby, H. *What's so Spiritual about your spiritual Gifts?* Oregon: Multnomah Publishers, Inc 2004

Carson, D. A. (1987). *Showing the Spirit: A Theological Exposition of 1 Corinthians 12-14*. Baker Academic.

Fee, G. D. (1996). *Paul, the Spirit, and the People of God*. Baker Academic.

Friedrich, G. (1973). *Theological dictionary of the New Testament, Vol. IX*. Wm. B. Eerdmans Publishing Company.

Kittel. Gerhard. *Theological Dictionary of the New Testament*. Grand Rapids, Michigan William B Germans Publishing Co.. 1968.

McRae, W. (1976). *The Dynamics of Spiritual Gifts*. Zondervan Publishing House.

Nygren, A. *Commentary on Romans*. Philadelphia Fortress Press, 1978.

Oliveira, E. *La iglesia Adventista frente al movimiento carismático*. Argentina: Casa Editora Sudamericana, 1975.

Packo, J. E. (1975). *Find and use your spiritual gifts*. Christian Publications.

Paulsen, J. *When the Spirit Descends Washington*. Review and Herald Publishing Association, 1977.

Sauer, E. *The Triumph of the Crucified*. Grand Rapids, Michigan: William B. Eerdmans Publishing Company, 1977

Stedman, R. *Body Life*. Glendale, California: Regal Books, 1979.

Storms, Sam. The Beginner's Guide to Spiritual Gifts. Ventura, California: Regal Books, 2002.

Stott, J. (1992). *The Authentic Church*. Editorial Certeza.

The SDA Bible Commentary. Washington: Review and Herald Publishing Association, 1957.

Turner, M. *The Holy Spirit and Spiritual Gifts – Then and Now*. Cambria, UK: Paternoster Press, 1999.

Valenzuela, A. (2005). *The Spiritual Gifts: Discover your mission in the Body of Christ. Living Ministry*.

Wagner, P. *Your Spiritual Gifts Can Help Your Church Grow*. Glendale, California: Regal Books, 1980.

Wagner, P. *Discover Your Spiritual Gifts*. Ventura, California: Regal Books, 2002

White, A. *Experiencias carismáticas en los comienzos de la historia Adventista.* Argentina: Casa Editora Sudamericana, sin fecha

White, E. G. (1892). *The Way to Christ.* Inter-American Publishing Association.

_____. (1898). *The Desire of Ages.* Pacific Press Publishing Company.

_____. (1904). *Testimonies for the Church*, vol. VIII. Inter-American Publishing Association.

_____. (1905). *Testimonies for the Church*, Vol. VIII. Pacific Press Publishing Association.

_____. (1911). *The Great Controversy.* Inter-American Publishing Association.

_____. (1941). *Christ's Object Lessons.* Washington: Review and Herald Publishing Asociation.

_____. (1970). *Consejos sobre mayordomía cristina.* Mountain View, California: Pacific Press.

_____. (1966). *Los hechos de los apóstoles.* Mountain View, California: Pacific Press.

_____. (1967). *Mensajes selectos.* Mountain View, California: Pacific Press.

_____. (1971) *Patriarcas y profetas.* Mountain View, CA: Pacific Press Publishing Association.

_____. (1962). *Primeros Escritos*. Mountain View, CA: Pacific Press Publishing Association.

_____. (1945). *Spiritual Gifts.* Washington: Review and Herald Publishing Association.

_____. (1948). *Testimonies for the Church*. Mountain View, California: Pacific Press.

Yohn, R. (1985). *Discover your spiritual gift and use it*. Tyndale House Publishers.

_____. (1980). *Discover Your Spiritual Gift and Use it*. Wheaton, IL: Tyndale House Publishers, Inc.

Notas

The Latter Rain: Unleashing the Gifts for the End Time!

Notas

www.ingramcontent.com/pod-product-compliance
Lightning Source LLC
Chambersburg PA
CBHW032004220426
43664CB00005B/141